TRIDENT K9 WARRIORS

TRIDENT
K9
WARRIORS

MY TALE FROM THE
TRAINING GROUND TO THE BATTLEFIELD
WITH ELITE NAVY SEAL CANINES

MIKE RITLAND

WITH GARY BROZEK

ST. MARTIN'S GRIFFIN ☙ NEW YORK

This is a true story, though some names and details have been changed.

TRIDENT K9 WARRIORS. Copyright © 2013 by Michael Ritland and Gary Brozek. All rights reserved. Printed in the United States of America. For information, address St. Martin's Press, 175 Fifth Avenue, New York, N.Y. 10010.

www.stmartins.com

All photographs except the following are courtesy of the author: Insert, page 16, middle: seals wcc.com.

The Library of Congress has cataloged the hardcover edition as follows:

Ritland, Mike.
    Navy SEAL K9 warriors : my tale from the training ground to the battlefield with elite Navy SEAL canines / Mike Ritland with Gary Brozek.—1st ed.
        p. cm.
    ISBN 978-1-250-02497-8 (hardcover)
    ISBN 978-1-250-02498-5 (e-book)
    1. Dogs—War use—United States.   2. United States. Navy. SEALs—Biography.   3. Dogs—War use—Iraq.   4. Dogs—War use—Afghanistan.   5. Iraq War, 2003–2011—Dogs.
6. Afghan War, 2001– —Dogs.   I. Brozek, Gary.   II. Title.
    UH100.R58 2013
    956.7044'345—dc23

                                                                                2013011252

ISBN 978-1-250-04181-4 (trade paperback)

St. Martin's Griffin books may be purchased for educational, business, or promotional use. For information on bulk purchases, please contact Macmillan Corporate and Premium Sales Department at 1-800-221-7945, extension 5442, or write specialmarkets@macmillan.com.

First St. Martin's Griffin Edition: January 2014

10 9 8 7 6 5 4 3 2 1

*This book is dedicated to the brotherhood, and
the loyal hounds that help keep them safe.*

ACKNOWLEDGMENTS

I would like to thank the following people, for without them this book would not have been possible.

My parents, George and Sandy—Thank you for putting up with me as a kid and instilling the values and foundation that forged me into the man I am today.

The SEAL Teams—Enlisting at eighteen, I grew up in the teams. There could not have been a finer collection of warriors to be around to set the example of how to live your life. The entire country owes you an infinite debt of gratitude for the violence you bestow on our enemies.

Marc Resnick, his assistant Kate Canfield, and everyone at St. Martin's Press—Thank you for your professionalism and pride in what you do. It's been a pleasure working with you.

Gary Brozek—Thank you for the countless hours of hard work you have put into this project, bringing my words to life in a way that couldn't make me prouder.

Brandon Webb—The brotherhood continues to prove that it takes care of its own, and your friendship and advice are certainly no exception. Thank you for everything, brother.

Wayne Dodge—Brother, there are no words to give ample thanks for what you have done for me, in more ways than one. Your friendship will be forever appreciated.

The warriors (both men and dogs) at MPC-1—You guys are the reason I do what I do, and I could not be prouder of the job you guys have done and continue to do.

Special thanks to:

The Allon Family	Cinnamon Bear
Happy	Johnny D
Fro	Mrs. Toad
BC	Mike Suttle
Mike Mike	Matt Betts
Wimbo	Darryl Richey
DK	
Shrek	
Del	
Echy	
Dusty	
CP	
SA	

AUTHOR'S NOTE

Since earliest recorded history, dating back to the time when humans first battled over territory or property using rocks and sticks, one other weapon has been used—canines. Whether it was the Ephesians doing battle, the Athenians fending off the advancing Persians at the Battle of Marathon, or the Spanish Conquistadors using Mastiffs against Native Americans, to more modern examples, we have utilized the dogs of war. Not only have they been utilized, they've been memorialized for their heroic loyalty and service. This book is my attempt to bring attention and praise to one segment of the military working dog community of warriors. At a time when an operator sitting in a room thousands of miles from a battlefield can direct a drone attack, when billions of dollars are spent developing high-tech weaponry, the one constant in war remains our use of canines. That speaks to their effectiveness as well as their heart, and proves the truth of their being Man's Best Friend.

INTRODUCTION

The tense silence was broken only by the sound of the MH-60's rotors and blades beating like a quickened pulse. Along with the sixteen other members of a West Coast–based SEAL Team, the multi-purpose K9 Duco sat vigilant and eager. Duco and his handler, Seth, had been assigned to a forward operating base (FOB) in northeastern Afghanistan, close to the Pakistani border in the mountainous region of the Hindu Kush. The area is well known as a porous zone where Taliban terrorists and their leaders travel from training grounds in Pakistan into Afghanistan. A few hours earlier Seth had attended a pre-mission briefing. The Operations Order commanded them to neutralize a high-value target in a nearby village, some fifty kilometers (thirty-one miles) away. The target, as the intelligence report had indicated, was a leading Taliban munitions expert, one of the head trainers who instructed cell leaders and their underlings in the deadly craft of improvised explosive device (IED) making.

With the communications check complete, Duco sat tucked between Seth's knees, his chest rising and falling at a slightly agitated rate as he reacted to the others' heightened sense of anticipation. The copilot radioed that they were several clicks from the landing zone (LZ). In their briefing, they'd learned that they'd have to fast-rope in; no LZ large enough or flat enough to accommodate three helos was in range. Seth stood and commanded Duco to do the same. Seth turned his back and waited. The platoon chief stepped forward and squatted in front of Duco before wrapping his arms around the dog's rear end and chest. Duco remained alert but impassive while he was being strapped into the harness on Seth's back.

Seth felt a *thwack* on his shoulder, a signal that he and Duco were good to go. Seth spent the next few moments making his way to the end of the line, checking the cams on his descenders, before stepping out of the MH-60's bay into the darkness. The only sound was the rush of wind past his ears and the high-pitched whirring sound of the rope snaking through the device. After unhooking the line, Seth waited for another team member to release Duco. He grabbed the dog's lead, double-checked the harness, and proceeded to the head of the formation. Behind him, the other men moved out of their defensive perimeter positions to follow Seth and Duco, all of them careful to maintain their spacing discipline. The SEAL Team members were all on comms, but Duco didn't need anyone to tell him what to do. All his years of training and experience, coupled with years of genetic fine tuning and his honed instincts, had been held at bay on the flight in and were now released.

Steadily moving at a pace between a lope and a trot, with his broad snout alternately to the ground and lifted above his shoulder to pick up any target odor, Duco worked along a snakelike path. He'd been trained to detect explosives and was at the head of the line sniffing out the possible locations of IEDs or munitions caches. His nose flaring and recessing like a beating heart, Duco led the platoon on into the night.

Even though it was pitch-dark, Seth and the others trusted that Duco's keen senses wouldn't fail him or them. They all may not have known that a dog's extraordinary *exteroception,* its ability to detect stimuli from the environment (including light, sound, chemical agents [taste and smell], heat, cold, and pressure), made the team members' night-vision goggles seem like tissue-roll binoculars by comparison, but they trusted Duco based on past experience. More than anything the bond of trust that existed between canine and soldier was once again being tested and ultimately proven worthy.

After several clicks maneuvering along a dirt road, Seth noticed something change in Duco's demeanor. The handler had anticipated seeing Duco signal that he'd detected the odor of explosives. Normally, if Duco had smelled explosives, he would have signaled detection by flagging his tail, hoisting it straight up and making it quiver from side to side, nearly like a rattlesnake alerting others to its presence. Along with that, he would become more intense, his movements more rapid, as he zeroed in on the exact location, his body acting as a kind of needle on a scale indicating that the concentration of molecules he was picking up was on the increase.

What Seth saw instead was Duco's body go rigid, assuming the posture of a show dog—head lifted, front shoulders at attention and stretched forward, his hips similarly straining forward. Seth also felt that strain on the leash and heard Duco emit a low whiny whimper.

Duco was letting the rest of the team know that they weren't alone.

Seth immediately called out, "Hey, Duco." The dog looked at him briefly and then resumed his intense staring into the darkness. Seth let the rest of the men know that he was releasing Duco. They knew there was only one reason for that: Duco had detected the presence of other humans. They immediately fell out and assumed an antiambush formation, finding cover behind rocks and trees. Seth waited a moment, touched Duco on the flank and felt the tautness of his muscles, and then unclipped the lead. He held him by the halter and whispered *"reviere,"* a word his original Dutch handlers used as a command to get a dog to search for a human. Seth released him. The dog eagerly sprang forward, dropping his back hips to give him more of a mechanical advantage to sprint, and then leapt.

Seth knew that Duco's eagerness was both bred into him and enhanced by training. In this scenario, detecting human scent meant the promise of being able to receive the ultimate reward, being able to bite down on something, in this case, human flesh. As human beings, we can exert 120 pounds of pressure per square inch with our jaws. A dog like Duco can nearly triple that number, remarkably approaching half the bite capability of a great white shark but paling in comparison to a hyena's 1,000 pounds and a crocodiles massive 2,500 pounds per square inch.

Seth and the other team members didn't know if that was part of the cultural distrust and loathing their enemy had for dogs, nor did they care. They also didn't sympathize with them when they heard the ferocious commotion coming from down a shallow embankment yards ahead of them. As the forward members of the team approached, they could hear shouts, snarls, and agonized screams. A few moments and a few bursts of gunfire later, and the night was dark and silent again, the stillness only broken by the one of the members saying, "Target is clear."

Duco emerged from the melee unscathed. Breathing slightly heavier, his head held high, he trotted back toward Seth. The handler knelt and clipped the dog back into his lead.

"*Braafy!*" Seth said, a word his Dutch handlers used in praise, as he pet him and ran has hand along his flanks. Duco curled into him and lifted his snout into the air. A few other men passed by, each thanking Duco with a "Get some!" a "Fuckin' A, son!" or some other sign of their praise and thanks. Duco sat there taking it all in, just another day at the office.

The rest of the team busied themselves with defending the perimeter, while a small group checked out the ambush nest. Along with the bodies of the four insurgents, they discovered a Russian PKM machine gun, several AK-47s, and hundreds of rounds of ammunition. After clearing the bodies from the site, they detonated the munitions and weapons. Four KIAs and a weapons cache destroyed was a good night's work for both men and dogs in war.

The dog lay in the shade of a stunted palm tree, his head up and his ears at attention. He was scanning the desert scrubland, vigilant, the lines of muscle beneath the heavy fur of his flanks taut and ready. Even from behind him, I could see his tongue lolling out of the side of his mouth, flopping like a pink fish.

"Duco," the man beside me said.

The Malinois, a Belgian herding dog, turned to look at us, his expression keenly alert and his dark eyes intent.

"*Heerre.*"

The dog sprang to his feet and made his way across the dusty terrain that passed for a yard in the desert communities well east of San Diego. Under other circumstances, I might have tensed up at the sight of this seventy-five-pound package of fierce determination approaching. As Duco neared, I could see recognition dawning; a nearly imperceptible softening of the muscles around his eyes let me know that he knew who I was.

He also knew enough not to approach me first, though the two of us had spent the first few months of his life in the United States together. As commanded, he came up to Seth, formerly his SEAL Team handler and now in his retirement Duco's caregiver, and sat alongside the man he'd served with on dozens of missions for the past six years. Duco sat, still very much at attention, until Seth told him it was okay.

Duco looked at me, and I noticed that the fur around his muzzle and eyes had lightened a bit and was no longer the deep ebony that had glowed like a spit-polished dress boot. What hadn't changed was the slight deflection in one line of the isosceles triangle of his large ears. Some scuffle as a pup in his kennel outside of Tilburg, in the Netherlands, had left him with an identifying mark. In my mind it wasn't a flaw, an imperfection, but a mark of distinction. I gave his head a few rubs with the flat of my hand and then ran it down his shoulder and along his rib cage. He was still in fine fighting trim, but I noticed that he relaxed out of his posture a bit and leaned into me. I smiled at this sign of affection and appreciation for the attention I was giving him.

"He's doing good," I said to Seth.

"Always. He's a good ol' boy." Seth pushed his sunglasses up and squinted into the distance. "He likes it here. Looks a little like the sandbox, but there's a lot less action. I think we both miss it—but don't at all."

Seth had spent more than a dozen years as a West Coast SEAL Team member, the last of it as a handler working with

Duco. Now they both spent their time together on a small ranch property outside of Ranchita, his property bordering on, fittingly enough, Hellhole Palms and the Anza-Borrego Desert State Park.

Having also served my time as a SEAL Team member and seen my share of action, I knew just exactly what Seth meant.

Now that I was working as a private contractor providing military working dogs (MWDs) to the navy and training them and their handlers, I was slightly removed from all that. Seth and Duco had ceased being active-duty military only three months earlier, and both would have chafed at the idea that they were "retired" and at all the associations we have of folks living in planned communities and riding around in golf carts or some such. Still, the transition for both man and dog isn't an easy one, and having trained SEAL Team members and their canine counterparts, I felt a deep empathy for both sides of the partnership. I can't really say that it was a formal part of my job or that it was written into my contract with the government that I pay these visits to my former trainees. It was a privilege and an honor, and more than that, a great pleasure to see them still together.

In most ways, Duco was still fitter and more capable than 99.9 percent of the dogs in this country, but that wasn't good enough for the kind of demands that he had to meet downrange in places like Afghanistan. Not only was the work so demanding but also the stakes were so high that anything less than the absolute best fell short of the requirement. It wasn't a question of heart. Duco still had the drive and determination, but the inevitable toll from age and years of stress was starting to creep in.

I knelt down alongside Duco and draped my arm around him. *"Braafy,"* I said. It always amazed me that something as simple as that short statement of approval meant so much to a dog, that over the years teams like Seth and Duco had developed such a bond of trust that the dog would willingly and gladly place himself in positions of peril.

A few minutes later, Seth and I sat down on the deck he'd recently built. Duco resumed his perimeter position in the shade. Seth told me a little bit about the enclosure he had built, split rail and wire, and he nodded out past the line of postholes he'd dug, the piles of dirt like overturned funnels flanking them.

"I'm not sure if I'm keeping the coyotes from getting in or Duco from getting out. I'm likely doing those varmints a favor either way. Duco would give them more than they bargained for, no doubt." Seth's voice still possessed a mild twang, revealing his Smoky Mountain roots.

"Damn straight he would."

"They wouldn't know what hit them."

Inevitably the talk turned to war stories. Seth shared with me an incident that forged the bond that existed between him and his dog.

"That time you took us out on that training exercise, doing the house-to-house maneuvers"—Seth shook his head and smiled—"he got hold of that target, and I thought I was going to have to choke him out to get him to release."

"They do like to bite," I said flatly, underscoring my understatement, "and Duco does more than most."

"I remember looking him in the eye, neither of us willing to give in, and then it dawned on that dog that he was the one who was going to give in, on account of me, and not because he wanted to. Then I knew I had him."

Seth went on to say that he believed that was the moment when he and Duco came to a better understanding. "I think of it this way: my daddy raised me to fear and respect him, and I did. But with what you helped us with, Duco obeyed because he got the idea that was the right thing to do and not 'cause I was going to beat his ass. Never in my life would I have thought a dog could communicate so much with a look and his posture."

"It doesn't always happen, but when it does, it almost defies explanation," I said.

"Hard work and love," Seth added, summing it up pretty nicely, I thought.

"Hey, Bud." Duco turned toward Seth, his eyes and ears alert. Seth smiled. "Good boy."

No matter that the navy had invested more than fifty thousand dollars in the acquisition, training, and care of Duco before Seth spent that year in our program pre-deployment, Duco was still "his." That was as it should be; unfortunately, it isn't always. I've trained hundreds of dogs for a variety of purposes, and it's not always easy to let them go to another home, especially a quality dog like Duco. Training dogs to be of service to us is my job, and it's also my passion. Seeing how a pair like Seth and Duco continue to operate does my heart good.

"I'd hate to think what would have happened if he wasn't with us," Seth said, echoing my thoughts exactly. "Instead, here we are."

There wasn't much I could say, so I didn't.

Seth set his beer down and reached into a wooden planter on the picnic table. He drew his lips back and let out a soft whistle. Duco stood, assumed the position, his ears tilting forward and pointing heavenward, his expression intent. Seth reared back and fired the tennis ball over the enclosure's fence and into the post-holed lot beyond. I watched as the ball arced and bounced wildly, and then I followed Seth's gaze from the ball's landing zone to the dog, no longer obscured in shadow but in the warm glow of the setting sun.

"Okay," Seth said at last.

Like a bow pulled tight and finally released, Duco shot out across the lot, kicking up dust. At the fence he didn't hesitate but easily bounded over the top rail, looking like a dressage champion horse at some grand prix. Duco had overcome a bunch of obstacles to become a distinguished member of our most elite Special Operations Forces (SOF), and it was good to see that he still surmounted them. I had to laugh as, in his eagerness, he stooped to clamp down on the ball and, his front legs splayed and his rear ones still churning, he nearly went, as my granddad might have said, "ass over teakettle."

His prize captured, Duco trotted back, munching on the ball, his mouth twisted into a kind of silly, giddy grin. He hopped the fence again and came onto the deck to show us what he'd managed to capture. He sat at Seth's feet, then lowered himself into a relaxed, paws-crossed lie-down, still working the tennis ball.

Seth looked at me half-embarrassed, half-pleased. "That's my one concession to his retirement."

I nodded, knowing that in training Duco would have been

told to drop the ball fairly quickly at his handler's feet. Those extra moments of reward, gnawing on that bit of felt and rubber, weren't all that he was getting. Seth stroked Duco's head, working his fingers around the backs of his ears as Duco cocked his head in pleasure.

Seth said, *"Los,"* and Duco released the ball.

Seth picked it up and offered it to me. I looked at the spit-frothed ball, it's optic yellow cover frosted in white, and declined.

Laughing, I said to Seth as he stood to throw another one for Duco, "Wilson. U.S. Open hard court. You've got expensive taste."

Settling back into his seat after letting Duco go bounding off to complete his appointed rounds, Seth sipped his beer and said, grinning with satisfaction, "Nothing but the best for my boy. He deserves it."

I couldn't agree more.

My trip to visit Duco and his handler wasn't just a social call. After having served in the U.S. Navy for almost thirteen years, eleven of which I spent as a SEAL Team member, since 2009 I've been training and providing working dogs for the military, various government agencies, and private individuals. Going to see Duco was a part of another responsibility that I take very seriously. I founded a nonprofit organization to make certain that retired military working dogs are able to live out the remainder of their lives in positive and beneficial environments. Though I knew that Duco was well cared for, I still wanted to check in on him, just like I frequently make contact with fellow members of SEAL Team 3, and members of other SEAL Teams I've come to know in my new role.

Whether you're a canine or a human, having been a SEAL Team member means you're a brother, and we are all our brothers' keepers for life.

By the time you finish reading this book, I hope you'll come to understand that there's not an ounce of disrespect intended when I make the comparison between what military working dogs in the SEAL Teams have contributed and what their human counterparts have done. Though the canines don't have as long a history as the humans—the SEAL Teams first utilized their own dogs a few years after 9/11—dogs and SEALs have occasionally worked side by side for decades. It wasn't until 2004 that the SEALs began to use dogs specially trained to meet the specific needs of the teams in-house. I'm proud to have been associated with the later development of dogs for use with the SEAL Teams specifi-cally and with the Special Operations Forces community generally. As you'll learn in the pages that follow, the training and implementation of dogs in combat has evolved over the years in the U.S. military. I'm especially proud of how the latest in training methodology has benefited both man and dog, made for more humane treatment of our animal broth-ers, and that the dogs operate in the field with tremendous courage and tenacity. These dogs have saved countless lives and prevented innumerable horrific injuries. As a nation, we owe them a tremendous debt of gratitude. By telling the story of some of these dogs, I hope to increase awareness of the vital role that military working dogs play, especially at a time of transition within our military.

Like most people, I knew that the military utilized dogs. Growing up, I'd seen enough war movies and viewed enough scenes of dogs held tightly leashed by handlers who were mostly members of the military police. While my knowledge of the role that dogs played in war evolved somewhat over the years, it didn't change much until I actually saw them in use in Iraq. There, I experienced one of those "lightbulb" moments, when I knew that the course of my life was going to see two paths joined together.

In April of 2003, a sixteen-member SEAL Team I was a part of was deployed to Iraq. This was the very early stage of the ground war, and we were tagging along with the First Marine Division. After a brief stay in Baghdad, we were tasked with taking the key city of Tikrit. Our convoy, consisting of twenty-five thousand U.S. Marines and my platoon, stretched out some thirty miles along the 119-mile route. Eventually we piggybacked with the Second Battalion and approached the city from the east, while other battalions (Light Armored Reconnaissance and Light Armored Vehicle) approached from the other cardinal directions. We spearheaded the approach, entering through a wealthy portion of the city near Saddam Hussein's palace. This was one of those hairs-on-the-back-of-your-neck-standing-up kinds of moments. The streets were deserted, and there was no sign of activity anywhere, but you knew that people were around despite the dead silence and the empty streets.

I experienced a similar kind of sensation, this time for a better reason, when we met limited resistance and took the palace down. The building was so massive, it took us more than an hour to clear all the rooms. We were there for four days and spent part of it on the roof of the palace, at the highest point in the city, overlooking the Tigris River. Beyond that lay the airfield where hundreds of pounds of cached weapons and munitions had been destroyed by the air force bombers with Joint Direct Attack Munitions (J-DAMs) and other smart bombs. As we sat on the roof, we watched sympathetic detonations, and at night it was like watching solar flares. Only this went on all day and all night, the explosive sounds and sights becoming the sound track to a once calm city now roiled by our munitions.

One night that stillness was broken by the sound of explosions close in—about 350 yards from our position. I was doing my four-hour block—between 0200 and 0600—when I saw three little flashes of light off in the distance and then a few seconds later those big explosions. The three flashes and then the explosions continued to our south, advancing to within 100 yards of the palace. As I was getting on the radio, I saw an army counter-artillery unit fire up across the Tigris, that movement accompanied by the sound of electric transformers, a mechanical *whizz-bang* electronic sound, followed by the sound of heavy weapons fire. In a matter of seconds those blips of lights we'd seen erupted in a massive flash, and whoever it was were wiped off the map. I sat there wondering what might have been. If those Iraqis had gotten their rounds off directed at us, who knows?

Those who-knows-what-might-have-happened questions are always a part of war, of course, and you don't spend a whole lot of time thinking about the answers. All I knew was that I was grateful that battery had been posted so nearby. Prior to our arrival in Tikrit, we'd stopped with the convoy for a bit to review the final stages of our entry into the city and had been ambushed. All hell broke loose during a fierce firefight, with antitank, antiaircraft rounds going off, the *whip-whip* sound of returned gunfire whizzing over our heads, and 84 mm rockets being launched into a field just outside the city. So we knew that despite the ghost-town appearance of Tikrit, there was plenty of resistance we might encounter. Who knew what we might discover in the city, and all our firepower, while certainly effective, might not be able to protect us from everything. As time went on, we had another weapon available to use that proved very valuable.

As the weeks passed, life took on a kind of routine—a combat normalcy that had you hypervigilant and never fully able to rest at any time. We had no forward operating base established, no outposts, and no real security perimeter established. We spent nights sleeping under Humvees and eventually set up tents beneath large camouflage netting hills we constructed. An hour of sleep here, a twenty-minute nap there was about all the shut-eye we got. For two months, I didn't shower, and nearly every moment was punctuated by gunfire, shouts, or some other disruption. We'd endured sleep deprivation before, but still, a toll was definitely being taken on us.

For that reason, and a lot of others, I was glad that a few weeks into our operation in Tikrit, several military working dogs joined those marines. At the time, as I've said before, the SEAL Teams didn't have our own dogs assigned to the teams. Some did serve with us, and they were essentially "borrowed" from other units. The clearing operations we were doing were particularly difficult. The potential for them to become mind-numbing was certainly there: the repetitive nature of them combined with the lack of sleep and other creature comforts contributed to that. But they were also highly dangerous and of critical importance.

At one point, we were in a more rural area outside the city, and I observed a small group of marines coming upon a small cavelike structure—a kind of hutlike thing with a very small entrance. I'd encountered other things similar to that one and had by that point searched thousands of buildings and other structures without any issues at all. The temptation would be to assume that all was okay, but we never gave in to that. This platoon had been assigned an explosive-detector dog, and he and his handler went up to that doorway. Immediately, the dog alerted: his ears went up and he sat down. I was on the security perimeter and watched all this through a pair of binoculars.

Later, talking to the marines who'd been investigating that cave, I learned that a grenade booby trap had been set in that doorway. Because of the way the structure was situated, and because of the way the explosives were placed, without question, two or three of those marines probably would have been killed—the first two or three guys going in. And the next one or two probably would have been injured fairly badly. That moment was literally and figuratively life changing.

Seeing for myself and then hearing more about how that dog just went about his business and instantly identified the danger made me want to never go anywhere without a dog out ahead of me ever again. Because it's so easy to place explosives, IEDs, booby traps, trip wires. At the pace that we were moving, it was impossible to sweep everything where you're going with a metal detector or have an Explosive Ordnance Disposal (EOD) guy pull open the ground. That's not going to happen. A metal detector doesn't cover everything anyway, because some of the devices use plastic or wood to house the explosives, so there is no metal. I also realized this: had there been somebody twenty feet inside that cave with an AK ready to shoot those marines as soon as they came in, the dog would have alerted them to that, too. I saw many other times how their ability to detect explosives and smell human beings and hear and smell things that aren't right was so far beyond my comprehension, it's incredible.

I also recognized something else about dogs that made them effective fighters. Unlike us, they didn't really act as though they were in a foreign environment. Call that naïveté or ignorance, but it worked to their advantage. In some respects they didn't know whether they were training here or over there, other than the exception of the constant and excessive loud noises. The mountains of Afghanistan or the deserts of Iraq aren't any more out of their routine locations than the mountains east of San Diego. The mountains are mountains, and there are steep jagged rocks, and they're searching for explosive odor, and they're getting to bite people, and they're doing what they were genetically designed to do. I already had some sense of just how that part of it worked, but like everything else, I didn't know how much I *didn't* know until I did it.

I also knew that I wanted to comprehend those abilities. I wanted to be able to harness their abilities and use them as an effective weapon against the tools of modern warfare. Eventually, that's what I did.

I'm a very lucky man in lots of ways. A lot of men and women haven't returned from our recent wars. I was able to, and even though a health issue forced me out of active duty overseas, I really enjoyed training SEALs before leaving the navy. Now, I combine two passions of mine—working with dogs and aiding in the defense of our country.

How a kid from Iowa whose best friend was a black Labrador named Bud eventually graduated from BUD/S and now works with the most elite fighting force in the world with the most elite four-legged fighting force today is a story worth telling. I believe many, many frogmen and other soldiers owe their lives to dogs that so loyally serve us and ask for comparatively little in return.

As I write this, I've got to take a break for a bit to tend to the dozen or so dogs I'm currently working with, as well as my own pets. The first thing you need to understand is that distinction between working dogs and pets. Like many people, I suspect, I wasn't aware early on just how much these dogs differed from others. All I knew was that from an early age, I liked dogs and, just as important, that I wanted a career in the military. Just as I'm thankful that we all benefit from military working dogs serving our country, I'm grateful that I've been able to combine into a career an interest in two things I care very deeply about.

— 2 —

Growing up in Waterloo, Iowa, I had a pretty typical suburban upbringing. I have two older brothers, Joe and Jake, and a younger sister, Lindsey. There was enough of a gap in our ages that, in some ways, we all kind of went our separate ways a bit—not that we weren't close, but in one regard we didn't completely share our love. We all pestered the hell out of my dad, George, and my mom, Sandy, about our desire to have a dog. Finally, when I was in the sixth grade, my parents came home with a black Labrador retriever puppy we gave the not-so-original name of Bud. We had friends and neighbors who had dogs—bird dogs and retrievers mostly—and I'd marveled at those dogs and their willingness to endure almost anything to get the job done. I joined friends duck and pheasant hunting, and seeing those dogs use their amazing athletic abilities and their desire to seek and retrieve fascinated me.

What motivated these dogs to put up with harsh temperatures, thick undergrowth, and other obstacles to get what
they wanted? Their drive and desire impressed the hell out
of me.

I couldn't get enough of hanging out with other people's
dogs until we got one of our own. As a result, I got to see
dogs in lots of different scenarios. I couldn't have known this
then, but that was the beginning of my education about canine behavior and the unique bond we've formed with that
species. At that point, I knew that I liked being around dogs,
but had no real thoughts about one day making my career
with them.

Though we lived in the suburbs of Waterloo, and with
nearby Cedar Falls there were about a hundred thousand
people in the surrounding communities, rural farm life wasn't
too far away. My dad's side of the family had a farm on the
outskirts of town. I spent a fair bit of time out there, riding
tractors, picking vegetables, and observing the various dogs
that lived on the farm. They weren't working dogs, strictly
speaking, but they weren't typical house pets, either. They
basically had to survive out on the farm on their own, and
they did a good job of it. From those hunting dogs and the
farm dogs, I developed the idea that canines should be useful and that they were often happiest when they had some
job to do—whether it was retrieving for a hunter or taking
down a critter for themselves.

I can still picture some of those farm dogs, trotting along,
their noses in the air, scenting for prey. They'd stop and go
stock-still and then pounce into two feet of snow and come
up with a field mouse or something else. The way they car-

ried themselves as they proudly toted their prizes said something about what was going on inside them. Of course, their drive to find prey had to be collared sometimes. I spent a lot of time dogproofing and shagging dogs away from the chicken coop. From my earliest exposure to dogs, I saw then that they had this drive to be of use and that they were genetically designed to be very good at tracking and at using their noses to guide them.

From the time Bud was old enough to walk a few hundred yards, to the time I left for the navy at the age of seventeen, I loved walking with him. Sometimes it was just those few hundred yards, and sometimes it was hours-long walks through the streets or with him in the fields with my dad hunting. Bud was, well, he was my boy. I'd come home from school everyday, and he would be there waiting for me, eager as all get out to go outside with me. I wasn't a complete loner, but I also wasn't the most gregarious kid around, so Bud and I spent a lot of time together, and I talked with him a lot, especially when I was younger. I loved sports but was a bit of a runt who didn't develop fully until after almost everybody else my age had, and I was somewhat self-conscious about that. Bud didn't ever seem to mind, and he never let me down, so that made him an even better companion.

That's not to say that he lacked the qualities of those good hunting dogs our neighbors and friends had. Just like them, Bud was able to detect different scents, and I was blown away by it. I would be out walking with him, and he'd do his usual nose-to-the-ground thing, occasionally rising up to sniff the air, and then all of a sudden he'd switch from going in one direction to moving in another. His entire demeanor would change, and he would run over to some area and start digging through layers of snow and ice to uncover some fast-food hamburger wrapper that had been buried there for who knows how long. That always fascinated me, the power of a dog's olfactory ability, even when it wasn't being used for the optimal purpose; at least from a human's perspective, it wasn't optimal.

I'd also see how a dog's intelligence could be optimized or let loose. With Bud, I saw his house smarts all the time, especially as it pertained to my grandma, Bev. Whenever she came by the house, Bud would grab something—a sock, a kitchen towel, the TV remote—and bring it to her. Why? Because she always rewarded him with a treat. Bud knew who the easy marks were, and he exploited that to his advantage. Even as a kid I sensed that if you gave a dog some of what he wanted, you could get a lot of what you wanted from the dog.

Dogs' companionship and loyalty and their purposefulness were entwined from the very beginning in my sense of their role in humans' lives. That didn't change, even when I was in the navy. I loved all those parts of their complex personalities. That's not to say that Bud was always 100 percent useful. I can still recall my dad coming into the door gimping pretty badly. Like a lot of Iowa males, he'd wrestled quite a bit and had bad knees and hips as a result of too many double-leg takedowns. As the story went, he was out with Bud at a local golf course that winter day, and Bud had a big head of steam and came charging at my dad in his exuberance. Bud clipped my dad and sent him sprawling. My father lay there in the snow, flat on his back, in pretty serious pain for quite a while. I remember wondering where the hell he and Bud had gone off to. Anybody who's ever had a big and energetic dog probably knows the drill, and my dad's lack of agility played into that.

What I like about that story is that Bud knew that something wasn't right, and he came and stood right by my dad, offering whatever consolation and comfort he could.

The point of all this is that I understand all sides of the human/dog equation. I love dogs as pets and companions. I admire them as workers and useful "tools," but I also know that left untrained and unguided, they can sometimes be annoyances. I feel sorry for anyone who hasn't experienced the joys of seeing a dog in action doing what nature intended, or even just the look in a dog's eyes when you scratch "that" spot for him or her. I appreciate all sides of the dog/human interaction enough that I've chosen to make training working dogs my career while still sharing my life with dogs as pets.

Even when I was still active duty in the navy with SEAL Team 3, I was heavily involved in the canine world. I owe my girlfriend at the time for setting me straight about a breed that has a notorious reputation in some circles. I have to admit that when she first told me that she had a female black brindle pit bull named Jada, my first reaction was, "Are you out of your fucking mind?" Within ten minutes, Jada had won me over with her intelligence and personality. She was the first pit bull I'd ever met in "canine," so to speak, and she really amazed me. Now, I'd been around working dogs and Bud and others until that point, but I'd never seen a dog that could change character so quickly. I was on post-deployment leave and was spending time with my girlfriend in Dallas, Texas. While she was at work, Jada and I got to spend time together. She was a friendly, playful girl whose intelligence was revealed in her wide inquisitive eyes. One morning, I saw the other side of Jada come out in full force.

We were walking along the sidewalk outside the apartment complex when a raccoon popped out from behind a row of garbage cans. It was a big sucker, about twenty-five to thirty pounds, and when it saw Jada, it reared up on its back legs and started hissing and emitting a demonic wail. Jada started to imitate the thing, except she crouched down low, and I could tell the two of them wanted to tangle with one another. I had Jada on a six-foot leash, and she was only about forty to forty-five pounds, but it took as much as I had to keep that dog from tearing away from me. Like an idiot, I figured if the two of them wanted to do what nature intended, then I wasn't going to get in the way. I let go of the leash. Jada took off and pile-drove that poor raccoon. Within about eight seconds, it looked as if that raccoon had been turned inside out. I was dumbfounded by how Jada had just flipped a switch and gone from that sweet little girl into the most aggressive dog I'd ever seen to that point.

I thought I'd seen some hard, bad-ass dogs before back in Iowa, ones willing to sit in a duck blind for hours, plough through chest-deep snow, and other things, but this was a revelation. Jada came trotting back to me without a scratch on her. I had visions of those poor old hunting dogs getting their snouts battered by some grumpy tomcat that sat back on its haunches like a boxer, leaning onto the ropes with paws flying. Jada would have made mincemeat out of those cats.

I realize I run the risk of perpetuating the negativity associated with pit bulls (what I call bulldogs) by telling this story.

I also don't use the word "pit" in describing American Pit Bull Terriers, because I despise the negative connotation to it. These dogs were bred to be hunters, and they are extraordinary at it. I've seen one of my dogs go after an enormous Russian boar, get flipped twenty feet away by the boar's horn, scramble back to its feet in an instant, and charge again. They have that kind of heart and courage.

Here's the point of my relating those events in Dallas. Jada exhibited a trait that nearly all of the many bulldogs I worked with after that had in spades. She had animal or prey aggression to a very high degree. She did not ever exhibit human aggression. In other words, her ferocity was directed at prey and not people. That's a crucial distinction, and I'll return to that point in a bit.

I was so impressed by Jada that I eventually really got into the bulldog world, owning as many as fifteen at a time, breeding them, training them, and doing small-game hunting with them as catch dogs, going after everything from raccoons and hogs to coyotes. The working-line bulldogs that I was involved with had animal aggression to a degree that I've seldom seen since, but they never, with one exception, ever went after humans. The lone exception was a bitch that, for the first ten days after giving birth to puppies, wouldn't let anyone near her pups. After those first ten days, she was fine with it. That's the only time any of the bulldogs I worked with ever showed any aggression toward a human.

I want to make this point as clear as possible: animals can demonstrate aggression toward other animals or toward people; but just because a dog is aggressive toward animals doesn't mean it has aggression toward people, and vice versa.

I believe there is a great misconception in our society over this point. There's no correlation between those two types of aggression. The dogs that we procure and train for the SEALs are all herding dogs—pointy-eared shepherds, usually Dutch shepherds or Belgian Malinois. These dogs are inherently human aggressive. That makes sense considering that they were bred to watch over flocks of animals. Through selective breeding, the herders that we "recruit" have had that human aggression tweaked to a very high degree out of necessity. Without the proper training and the control of a well-trained handler, these dogs would be a potential threat to folks.

I point this fact out as one way to illustrate how the military working dogs that accompany the Navy SEALs are not like the average pet in several ways. That human aggression component is probably the most obvious, but there are other ways in which these dogs are not your typical house pets, no matter how well-bred those dogs might be. These dogs are also highly motivated and extremely energetic. One way to put this into context is for you to think of the most ball-crazy dog you've ever seen. You know the type—the one who will pursue a ball faster, for greater amounts of time, and with a maniacal determination that has you shaking your head or getting rotator-cuff surgery after throwing or flinging a ball for too many hours a day to satisfy its craving.

The dogs that make it through the program and qualify to join the SEAL Teams on their missions are head and shoulders above anything you've seen. The analogy I often use to describe the difference is this: a lot of people want to be professional athletes. They start playing a game early in their childhood; a few become big-deal high school athletes, may make it into college; and a very, very small percentage realize that dream and play professionally. The analogy doesn't end there. From that select group who make it into Major League Baseball, the National Basketball Association, the National Football League, or whatever other pro sport, an even more minute percentage become stars, Hall of Famers, legends. Every dog we work with has the same advantages and skills that those acclaimed athletes have. They are not genetic freaks, because of the carefully programmed and designed selection of traits and breeding pairs, but they are as physically gifted as a Michael Jordan or a Michael Phelps.

Phelps is a good example. I started swimming competitively at the age of five with the Waterloo Sharks swim club. By ninth grade, I was all of five feet, four inches tall and weighed 105 pounds. Michael Phelps, by comparison, is six feet, three inches tall and weighs approximately 180 pounds. Combine that with his six-feet, seven-inches arm span, he is a marvel of swimming efficiency. Some of that he worked on, some of that he was given. That's how it is with our dogs. We start with the best genetic makeup we can and then hope to be able to best utilize those traits. Obviously, great athletes are great for reasons other than their physical gifts. They are frequently tenacious competitors, driven by some inner mechanism that wants to not just succeed but dominate. That doesn't mean that they are arrogant or malicious: they just want to be better than you or anyone else.

The Belgian Malinois that I've worked with have to have that component. It's not enough to be well-bred. They have to have some inner fire that you can control and unleash to the best advantage. The reason why we use Belgian Malinois is that they combine two essential qualities needed to be a multi-purpose dog that is of use to the Navy SEALs. They have a highly developed sense of smell, and they possess a strong willingness to be assertive and to bite. They have a lot of other great attributes. Their athleticism and endurance are extraordinary, and their fearsome appearance certainly helps in some regards, but since their primary tasks are to detect specific odors and to assist in capturing bad guys, their ability and willingness to do those two things make them ideal candidates. And I don't just mean they have those two traits; they have them in spades—particularly the dogs who make the grade and get deployed in theater.

Here's another way to think about this: some dogs are obsessed with squirrels. They'll go after them hard, tree them, and then sit there and stare up into the limbs at them. They may bark and jump at the trunk for a while, but eventually they'll give up. The kind of prey aggression that we look for will mean that that dog will persist far longer at the task of getting that squirrel than any other dog. They will be relentless about it to the point of annoyance, except that's exactly what we're looking for in them. We want dogs that exhibit traits that would drive most owners out of their minds. We want the over-the-top, extreme "prey drive." They have to be bold, powerful, stubborn, type A, and dominant. In addition, and perhaps most important, they have to be absolutely crazy to retrieve things.

Since most of the work these dogs do is detection work—finding people, explosives, narcotics, and other things—they also have to have a good nose. That's why, despite my admiration for what bulldogs can do, they typically aren't a good fit for the primary missions that military working dogs are assigned. Herding dogs are superior trackers in comparison to bulldogs. Hounds (bloodhounds in particular) are extraordinary trackers but lack the prey or human aggressiveness that the Belgian Malinois possess. The same is true with retrievers. Labradors make great drug-sniffing, explosive- and munitions-detection dogs, and so on; they just don't have the same human aggression component that is necessary to meet the SEAL Teams' needs.

Having a good nose isn't even enough for a herding dog. They have to have the desire to chase. From the very beginning, when I work with pups even before they are whelped, I look for that tenacious desire and also feed into it. Whether you take a piece of PVC pipe, pieces of copper tubing, chunks of wood, a tennis ball, a rolled-up towel, rags, or whatever, when you wave it in a potential working dog's face, it better go after it and not be distracted or lose interest after a little while.

Again, the point is this: all dogs have to one degree or another the traits we look for. Very few dogs have the combination of traits I've mentioned (plus things like great cardiovascular capability, a strong bite, and the adaptability to deal with a large number of environments and stimuli and not be too fearful or too curious) all in one package and to the degree the work they do demands.

Another way I've explained this to people is to say that the Navy SEAL dogs have to be like the human members of the teams. The drop-out rate among those who want to qualify as a Navy SEAL is very high. The drop-out rate among the dogs we select and train is even higher than that.

I have read stories of dogs that were abandoned and placed in shelters and that eventually became military working dogs. That's the exception to the rule. Just like there are more than a few "mutts" who transformed themselves and earned the coveted trident insignia as a SEAL Team member, so can some dogs. The reason why we travel all over the world to select dogs to bring to the United States for additional training is because the time and money that our government and the military have to invest in these dogs is considerable. We want to start with the best platform that we can, and the long-standing, carefully monitored bloodlines of the European dogs is one kind of shortcut that we generally use. It would take generations and countless dollars to begin a selective breeding program using those bloodlines here in the United States. This is a matter of expediency and necessity. We'd rather sacrifice the MADE IN THE USA label than potentially lose American lives or waste taxpayer dollars. We all want the best for our troops, and at this point, the best means importing these dogs from overseas.

The Belgian Malinois gets its name from both the country (Belgium) and the city (Malines) where they were first bred. Their origins go back beyond 1891, but the first dog registered in Belgium and the neighboring country of France as a Chien de Berger Belge was born that year. Many of the dogs of this breed are fawn colored (beige) with a black mask. That's not true of all four varieties, which are distinguished by their coat, ranging from short to long in length, smooth to rough in texture, and from fawn to black in color. I've worked with all four members of the breed type, and all are desirable as military working dogs.

A dedicated early group of breeders and trainers refined the breed so that it is prized for its abilities as a working dog as well as one that excels in various kinds of field-trial competitions. According to the American Kennel Club, Belgian Malinois were first registered in the United States in 1911, but the numbers of them in the United States were so low that, before 1959, in AKC competitions they were lumped into the "miscellaneous" category. To give you some idea of how rare they were in the United States, and to a certain extent still are, only 107 dogs were registered in the ten years after 1959. Today, they remain one of the smallest breeds, numerically, in the AKC.[1] They have always been well regarded for their intelligence, trainability, and their willingness to work as herders, in pulling, and in tracking. Because they are relatively rare here and have a long history of breeding, training, and competing in Europe, we most often import dogs from there. They enjoy a nearly fanatical following in the United States, and while there are some very good breeders and trainers domestically, we want the best of the best, and that means utilizing those long ancestral lines and the rich tradition found in dogs from Belgium and Holland and elsewhere. They served their countries in two worldwide conflicts, and they continue to honor their breed's history in how they perform in support of U.S. troops today.

3

I can easily back up my claim that the comparison between the types of dogs needed and used in the Special Operations Forces community and the types of people needed and used are much the same. Obviously, the comparison does break down in some areas, but the degree to which the canine and human components are alike is highly significant. Having been involved in all sides of this, as a SEAL Team member, as a SEAL Team trainer, as a breeder of dogs, and as a trainer of dogs that I've purchased for use in the SOF field, I think I'm qualified to make that assessment. Other trainers may quibble with some of my methodologies and opinions, but I believe the results speak for themselves. My clients/customers are very satisfied with the dogs I've provided them for a variety of uses, and that's especially true of the dogs that have been placed with the SEAL Teams.

One of the areas in which the comparison between the dogs and the humans in the SEAL Team members breaks down immediately and definitively is in breeding. As humans, we don't have a formal and scientific kind of breeding program that produces SEAL Team members. I know from my own experience that the men I worked and served with as a member of SEAL Team 3 were an incredibly diverse bunch of guys. We did have some things in common: many of us were raised in either suburban or rural environments, liked doing things that are often referred to as "outdoor enthusiast" activities—hunting, fishing, climbing, hiking, and so on. Almost all of us played some sort of organized sports. Guys with backgrounds like that are in the majority, but they're not exclusively of that "type."

But there were also enough guys I met in my time who made you pause and ask, "You did *what* before joining up?" For example, in my first platoon, there was a guy that was an Ivy Leaguer—a Columbia grad—who was a Wall Street investor for several years, got bored, and decided to quit, joined the navy at thirty-one years old, and went through BUD/S. I'd also been on a team with a guy who'd been a rodeo clown previously. Another guy was a pothead, followed the Grateful Dead, and for a number of years was a professional skier—a ski-patrol member, ski guide, and instructor. And then in the summertime he was a white-water raft guide on the Colorado River. He did that for a number of years and then he got tired of it and decided he wanted to join the navy and become a frogman.

Obviously, none of us were purposely bred to have an interest in any of those things; we either developed those interests ourselves or had family members or other expo-sures in our environment that led us to them. In my case, both my grandfathers served in World War II, one in the army and one in the navy. I was always fascinated by the sto-ries they told me about their service during that war. They were a part of the "Greatest Generation," and they had some of those traits—unquestioning loyalty, dedication, and humility among them. They didn't talk much about their war experiences, but I was eager to hear anything about them, and they obliged me. It seemed like few others in my family really were as interested, but for some reason, I was. I became fascinated—"obsessed" might be a better word—with the idea of becoming a navy frogman after reading an article about them and the incredible challenge of SEAL training in *Popular Mechanics* magazine. Also, the movie *Navy SEALs* was an effective recruiting tool for me and a number of other guys in the teams.

All of this to say that you never know who is going to make it as a SEAL, let alone who might be drawn to this life. Not all of it is random, but in my case, my level of interest and a somewhat random event combined to inspire me. Be-cause of my grandfathers' and my father's influence (though he didn't serve), I was raised to believe that you should be proud to be an American and that you can do a lot more than just express that pride verbally. Wanting to go out into the world and do something active for my country was my re-sponse to those stories I'd heard and the words and images I'd seen. Not everyone has that kind of response, and I can't fully explain why I did. I also had a highly refined sense of right and wrong instilled in me.

That sense came into play in particular in January of 1992. January 6, 1992, to be precise. It was a Friday afternoon, and I was a freshman in high school. I was a member of the swim team, a newbie, and as part of an initiation ritual I was required to wear my Speedo swimsuit over my jeans. Maybe that made me a target of a racially motivated attack at school. In March of 1991, the Rodney King beating had sparked a fair bit of racial tension nationwide, and my high school was no exception. King was the Los Angeles man who was severely beaten by members of the Los Angeles Police Department who were eventually acquitted of any wrongdoing a couple of months later. Our high school, Waterloo West, was racially mixed, and there were some tensions right before this about a Cultural Enrichment Club meeting being canceled because some white students promised to show up to it and cause problems.

I was walking to class, just after having lunch with my older brother, Jake, when I ran into a gauntlet of black students. Wrong place at the wrong time, I guess. I was beaten up pretty badly, and I hated the feeling of powerlessness I experienced in those moments when I was punched, kicked, and slammed into the walls. *No* action was taken against the guys who beat the shit out of me. *I* took some action. I told myself that I would never again experience that kind of helplessness. I joined a local dojo, led by a sensei who had a very old-school mentality of what was what. It was everything a martial arts school should be, one that unfortunately rarely exists these days. My sensei's mentor served in Vietnam as a Force Recon Marine, and I was naturally very interested in his experiences in combat. I became committed to defending myself in ways other than just some street-fighting moves that were learned the hard way. While I couldn't have connected all these dots back then, that desire dovetailed with what I later saw as the role of the United States—to protect and defend against aggressors and other kinds of bullies.

Add all of those influences up, as well as a best friend named Matt who shared a similar interest and work ethic, and I was fully committed to joining the military right out of high school and chose the navy and the SEAL Teams as my aspiration.

I tell this story because it demonstrates some of the points I want to make about dogs and humans and breeding and training and the unpredictable nature of it. I was predisposed to becoming a SEAL; that beating incident could have led me another way altogether, but it didn't. I wasn't "bred" to be a SEAL, and at that point, I wasn't exactly the model physical specimen you might imagine a SEAL Team member being. I was the typical late bloomer physically, but at the time I was the kind of Charles Atlas type, not exactly a ninety-pound weakling, but I was drawn to fitness and the discipline—mental and spiritual—of the martial arts.

If I did possess one trait "out of the box," so to speak, that made me a prime candidate for a SEAL Team member, it was this: I was ultra-competitive. I hated to lose, and as much as I felt helpless during that attack, by virtue of being so outnumbered, I also recoiled at the idea that, in my mind, I should have been able to overcome those odds. My fantasy was typically adolescent: I would have been jumped and then been able to fight my way out of it, breaking jaws and knocking out teeth along the way. I should have been able

to overcome the numbers, and that is what separates successful SEAL Team candidates and is the one trait that I would
say we all had in common despite our divergent upbringings.
SEAL Team members don't want to lose, and they won't ever
quit. Ever.

In finding, breeding, selecting, and training dogs, I have
to say that the same trait is necessary. The single most desirable trait in a dog that will do SOF work is this: they won't
quit. Combine that with some of the other required physical
characteristics of a dog, and you've got yourself a prime candidate to do the necessary work of the SEAL Teams.

Sometimes their willingness to go anywhere and do anything ends up being a kind of detriment. That's especially true
when they are "fresh out of the kennel" at the beginning of
their training with us, and are being exposed to new activities
and new environments. I'm painfully aware of this fact.

Ask any West Coast SEAL what he thinks about the
manzanita bush, and most of what they have to say isn't
something I could repeat here without blushing a bit. The
San Diego County region of the United States is ripe with
the stuff. *Manzanita* means "little apple" in Spanish, but most
of us who've endured the agony of working our way through,
around, under, and away from its thorny grasp think of it as
more of a man-eater than an apple bearer. Because the dogs
we train come from Europe, none of them have had experience dealing with the nuisance that manzanita brings.
Belgium isn't exactly a high-desert mountainous region, so
one of the environments that we have to expose the dogs to,
which is very much like Afghanistan, is in Southern California near the West Coast SEAL Teams.

As a SEAL, you get exposed to manzanita during night patrols, and it is about the thickest, coarsest, sharpest vegetation that you'll ever encounter. When we train the dogs to do mountain patrols at night, you wish that maybe these dogs didn't have that all-speed-ahead spirit. One dog in particular, Barco, was one of our larger specimens, weighing in at eighty pounds. He is a freight train with a brain. Sometimes, however, that locomotive engine in him overpowers the driver.

We were on a night training exercise, and Barco was on a thirty-foot retractable leash, a heavy-duty flexi-lead. Short leads are effective in some scenarios, but when training a dog to do detection work in the mountains, something that short just isn't practical or realistic to use. If you've ever walked your dog and had the frustration of him or her going around a tree and wrapping the lead around it, you've experienced something like what we've endured. Imagine if instead of your mild-mannered dog on a short leash winding around an oak tree with its relatively smooth bark, you've got an eighty-pound, high-energy beast intent on getting to an odor so that he can be rewarded by being able to play with his favorite thing in the whole world. And that tree isn't a smooth oak but a torturous manzanita. And your outing isn't along a sidewalk in a subdivision or city but is in the mountains. And your nighttime walk isn't aided by streetlights, but you're in pitch-blackness in the middle of the mountains. A classic recipe for disaster.

Barco had a real talent for forging ahead, wrapping back around a manzanita bush, doubling back, coming around again, straining against his lead, and wrapping that bit of fabric tighter and tighter. I've been out on training exercises with a group of six to eight dog and handler teams and this is supposed to be done in stealth—and every few seconds you'd hear another handler muttering "son of a bitch," and much worse, when one dog after another got tangled up in a man-eating bush.

Of course, I don't mean that literally, but almost. One night, I was out with Barco and a few others, and we came to a downhill section, and Barco was on point. He took off like a shot, and suddenly we were in the middle of an old Holly-wood western, where a cowboy is being dragged by his horse or behind a wagon or whatever. His handler, who shall re-main nameless, went down the hill like a rag doll, gravity and Barco determining his speed and direction, bumping along and kicking up a cloud of dust. I went down the hill after them as quickly as I could, but not soon enough to prevent the handler from getting hung up upside down in a prickly bush. Barco's forward progress was only arrested because his handler's limbs were entwined within that tangled manza-nita. Each of Barco's continued thrusts forward impaled his handler into the sharp points and further knotted the lead, producing tension in it that required many minutes of patient undoing to free man and beast.

Sometimes it isn't because of the dog's over-the-top (but desirable when controlled) eagerness that gets handlers in trouble. Sometimes they are their own worst enemies. Ball rewards are what keep these dogs motivated. Once, Matt and his dog Arras were on a night patrol, and Arras indicated properly when he came to an odor by sitting still and staring at it. To reward him for properly detecting and indicating,

Matt thought it was a good idea to toss Arras a ball. Of course, Matt forgot that it was nighttime. He had on his night-vision goggles, and while dogs can see well at night, Arras didn't catch sight of the ball immediately, so he didn't make the catch. Instead, he heard it hit off some rock and bounce down the slope. Keep in mind that we were at the top of a 4,800-foot mountain. Arras took off and Matt soon followed, swept off his feet and progressing down the rocky slope at a rate considerably faster than when he'd struggled up it moments before.

I think incidents like these are teachable moments, and so when you get your lightly bloodied and battered handler back near you, you remind him that in certain situations, it's best to get the dog right by your side where you can hand it its reward. With dogs and humans, it's all a learning process. Few of our handlers have any experience with dogs that have the physical gifts and enormous drive that our future multi-purpose K9s do. They have to learn about this the hard way all too frequently.

I mention this physical component only briefly, but it is obviously important. It's a given that a dog has to be healthy and fit, but it is more their temperament that sorts them out in the final analysis. Their physicality is important in another way; for example, the weight difference between the German shepherd dog and the Belgian Malinois is a crucial factor in our decision to employ them as SEAL Team members. The ten pounds less that a typical Malinois weighs make a big difference for a handler in the field as he lifts the animal dozens of times a day.

This is similar to what goes on in the military. The navy does a physical screening early on and will eliminate from consideration anyone who has an obvious physical disability or other potential health issue that would hinder that person's ability to do the job required of them. A relatively small number of people are eliminated at that stage. What's also true of humans is that sometimes their physical traits prevent them from being able to perform specific tasks. As a kid, I remember reading stories and watching movies and documentaries about World War II aviators. The ball turret gunner, the man who rode in a glass bubble slung from the belly of the bomber, had to by necessity be a small man. Therefore, someone's height could disqualify him from performing that task. That doesn't mean that they weren't capable of being good servicemen; they just couldn't do that specific job. That's much like the situation with the Malinois. Many other breeds of dogs do valuable work for our government, but some just don't qualify as SOF/SEAL Team members because of some physical trait.

I want to take a moment to discuss my use of some terminology. In the mind of the military higher-ups, broadly speaking, a dog is not a SEAL Team member. In the strictest sense, dogs are accounted for in the same way that a piece of equipment is. There is a movement among the military and other canine advocates to eliminate that designation and to treat dogs not in the same manner as humans but in a manner that better fits with what they do for us and how they serve the country. A dog shouldn't just be a line item on a budget sheet along with a weapon, a vehicle, or an office supply. What they do is far more important and far more complicated than that. I think it's important to get into this, but I would like to say that back during Vietnam the brass thought of dogs as equipment, and now the military treats the dogs as counterparts to the operators—from medevacing wounded dogs, rehabbing injured dogs, to awarding medals and ribbons and holding memorials for fallen KIA dogs.

Another analogy to consider when thinking about this canine-versus-human comparison is what happens after basic training is completed and the evaluation for suitable candidates for SEAL Teams begins. In my case, I knew going in that I wanted to be a SEAL, and I let the recruiters know that was the case. Not that my desire mattered much, but when it came time for me to take the preliminary screening test, I was well ahead of the game. Because I was so highly motivated, I'd been working out twice a day, six days a week, for a long time before reporting to Great Lakes Naval Training Center. In fact, I thought that basic training was a detriment rather than a benefit for someone like me. The physical training was so less intense than what I was used to doing that I felt like my fitness level was suffering.

Two weeks into basic training, I did take that fitness test—a five-hundred-yard swim, the maximum number of sit-ups and push-ups in a two-minute span for each, six dead-hang pull-ups, and a mile-and-a-half run. I easily outdid the minimum numbers. Fortunately, that allowed me and others like me to do additional workouts and to have access to the fitness facilities after I passed that first assessment.

Had I not passed that assessment—and I was the only one

of the eight or nine in my division who attempted it—I wouldn't have been bounced out of the navy, but I would have felt like I had been. The screening was a breeze, and I knew that I had a lot more to look forward to when the actual BUD/S training began. That was to be a ways off, but I was eager to get there.

Similarly, when I travel to Europe to begin my screening process to select dogs to bring back to the United States to train for SEAL Teams, they've already gone through some initial training, have been bred to heighten certain traits, and have that crucial "drive" trait in spades. I put the word "drive" in quotation marks because it raises questions about dogs and their emotions. Absolutely, dogs do have emotions. Do they have the same spectrum of emotions that we do?

No.

Do they have "drive"?

Absolutely.

If you've ever been around a dog, you know that they want certain things. Besides the quality of not being likely to quit easily, the second trait that I look for in dogs is their drive. Call it enthusiasm, tenacity, or whatever, but, like a coach looking to recruit an athlete, you want to see that drive demonstrated. It is the combination of their unwillingness to quit and their willingness to go after something *unrelentingly* that I look for when evaluating dogs. That may seem redundant or hairsplitting, but the examples that follow should shed some light on the differences between not quitting and really going after it.

For most pet owners, the drive I'm talking about can best be observed when you have in your possession a favorite toy that your dog likes to play with. For a lot of dogs, the toy of choice is a tennis ball. When I go to look at dogs, physically mature dogs in most cases, what I want to see are behaviors that would drive most pet owners nuts. The dog should express its desire in leaping, barking, turning, and spinning. And I don't just mean the dog does that for a little while, but persistently, for a long duration. Their desire must be over the top, and they almost literally exhibit that trait by jumping up to nearly my eye level to get to that ball. They are, as I said, relentless in that pursuit of the ball and would very definitely cross the line between what we consider acceptable and unacceptable pet behavior. I want to see a dog that is willing and able to use its only real weapon—its mouth—to get that ball. Simply put, they have so much desire and are so unwilling to give in and lose the battle for that ball that they will bite a human to get it.

If you've ever seen a dog that just shivers with excitement and pent-up desire to get a toy, then you have some idea of what I'm talking about. It's as if every fiber of its being is twitching with its genetic desire to get at prey. For the dogs at the top of my list, the object of their desire is nearly immaterial. I could be holding a piece of pipe, a length of rebar, a stick—it doesn't matter. They want it and will do nearly anything to get it. They are so highly motivated that it is nearly impossible to describe their behaviors. In addition to wanting it while it's in your possession, they will tear off after it at high speed as soon as the object leaves your hand when you throw it. Their aggressive pursuit of that object, the speed at which they go after it, is again at the very top of the charts. To say that they take off after it is an understatement; they

launch themselves. After that, when they arrive at their destination, they crash the ball, planting their forelegs so force-
fully that their hind legs rise up off the ground, kicking up
dust and debris all over the place. They will then grab it,
wrap it up with front legs and paws around it, and then go
into a guarding position, not allowing anyone near it.

Compare that response to your typical ball-obsessed dog,
and I think you get the picture.

If you manage to approach the dog and try to take the
object away, the only way you'll get it is if you come close to
choking the dog into unconsciousness. Again, that's not what
you want out of your pet, but it is absolutely what we want
out of a dog that can do the job with a SEAL Team. Of course,
I'm talking about their raw "skills" at this point. Eventually,
that dog will have to be trained to behave this way only on
command, though—as I'll deal with in more detail in the
next chapter on training—there's a fine line between taking
that kind of prey drive out of a dog and managing that prey
drive. Prey drive is the ability and desire to chase and catch
anything that moves. What I'm looking for, as I've said, is
over-the-top prey drive.

I've taken clients who want a personal-protection dog to
view candidates, and when they see that kind of behavior,
they frequently say, "Is there something wrong with that
dog?"

I always say, "No. There's a lot right about that dog."

The reason why that kind of nearly out-of-control pursuit
is needed is because frequently these working dogs, once in
the field, have to charge into an unknown environment and,
just as frequently, one that presents a real danger to the dog.

You don't want a dog that is going to hesitate at all and give a single thought to its safety. You just want them to get in there and do the job. Apprehending a bad guy is just one task that these dogs are trained to do, and it is an important component of SEAL Team work. Some dogs have that great prey drive and pursuit, but they may be lacking in a second skill that is required of SEAL Team dogs but may not be required to work for other agencies.

The second type of job is detection. Dogs are legendary for the sensitivity of their noses, and for good reason. I frequently say when describing what I'm looking for in a dog that I want a nose and the rest of the dog that comes with it doesn't really matter. That's not literally true, of course, but it comes close to describing the priority placed on a dog's olfactory ability. I term a dog's ability and desire to find an object that isn't visible their "hunt drive." That means that whether an object is thrown into an area where the dog can't see it or was hidden previously, I want to see that dog use its nose and not its eyes to locate that object. Just as the dog has to possess a hyper prey drive, the ideal canine candidate has to possess a hyper hunt drive.

Instinctively, these dogs should immediately go into a serpentine-shaped search pattern or a figure eight. Their noses will either be lowered or up in the air scenting, using the wind and the scent molecules to locate the object. Just as when they chase and capture something they've seen thrown, their hunt drive will turn into aggressive possession once they have the object.

As rare as it is to find a dog with the kind of prey drive that we seek, it is equally difficult to find a dog with the kind of nose that will help it succeed as a working dog with the SEAL Teams. Finding a dog with both those qualities is truly a one-in-a-thousand (or more) proposition. That's where good breeding comes in, of course, and selecting for both those traits will invariably produce dogs that are stronger in one area over another. That's okay, but the difference can't be so great that the dogs are inferior in one of those areas. The SEAL Teams, unlike some other agencies, have to employ dual-purpose dogs—those that excel at apprehension and detection. By necessity, then, you might make some concessions that you may not make with a single-purpose dog.

In baseball, scouts look for five-tool players: those who can hit for average, hit for power, and who possess a strong throwing arm, above-average foot speed, and a good glove. No player has ever been at the top of the charts in every one of those categories, but they are above the average. To keep the baseball analogy going a little bit longer, what we need are first-ballot Hall of Famers who are in the ninetieth percentile in all the skills we look for.

One of the traits that allows a dog to be relentless in its prey and hunt drives is its ability to block out distractions. Whether that distraction takes the form of a squirrel, a helicopter, gunfire, or any other stimulus from their environment, it absolutely must remain task focused. In addition to that, it has to enter into a new environment for the first time and not be intimidated. In fact, it has to be the opposite of intimidated. Its upright carriage, its scorpion tail curling over its back, its pricked ears, and its chest thrust forward have to be a constant no matter the environmental distractions or the foreignness or its unfamiliarity with a locale.

Again, I don't want to diminish the respect that I have for dogs kept as pets. For example, there are many, many fine hunting dogs that grow accustomed to the sound of gunfire. There are many dogs that are "ball crazy" and indefatigable pursuers of objects and animals. The ones that we deploy have to be unflappable in all circumstances; they can't be spooked by dark rooms, slippery floors, open metal grating, helicopters, fast roping, rappelling, parachuting, entering and exiting water, jumping onto unstable objects, or entering tight places like ducts and crawl spaces. Not only can't they be spooked, they have to go into those places and perform their activities willingly and with a single-minded purposefulness that few if any humans possess. In other words, they need to stroll in everywhere like they own the place, just like us frogmen.

The last quality that I look for is difficult to describe in delicate terms. A dog has to have a big set of nuts on him— metaphorically speaking. Most dogs, even among those selected from the elite breeders from around the world, don't have the kind of dominance and true forward aggression that is needed. Dogs have been domesticated and bred for so long that the type of dog that is willing to stand up to and fight a human—a human that is not frightened by that dog and physically capable of disabling that dog—is a very, very rare animal. I call them the 1 percenters (this was before the term had a political connotation), but they are more like one in ten thousand.

To test for that rarest of qualities, I have to put the dog in an uncomfortable spot and put pressure on him. Essentially, what I'm testing for is its fight-or-flight response. I want to see it go through that thought process: *Am I going to take this guy on? I know that chances are that I'm going to get hurt if I do, so I could bail out.* The ones that don't bail out, the ones that choose to fight and not flee, are the ones I want.

In evaluating dogs for purchase and further training, I do have an advantage when it comes to testing for this kind of aggressive behavior. They've never seen me before, so I immediately have their attention as a potential threat. When I put additional pressure on them, by approaching them, by keeping my body square to them with fierce direct eye contact, and by presenting a stick as a weapon (in some cases) and tapping them with it or by grabbing a handful of their skin and squeezing it, I want them to come after me. Of course, I'm wearing a "bite suit" for protection when I do this, and the dogs that use that bite suit for its intended purpose are good candidates for selection.

It's important to note that there is a crucial distinction between dogs that will go on the offensive and those that will continue to fight when placed on the defensive. A dog may demonstrate prey drive when going after a squirrel, but one that will exhibit that same prey drive when squaring off with a moose or other large animal are rare and desirable as working dogs.

The men who qualify for the SEAL Teams possess many of those same basic traits as the dogs we train. A good nose is not one of them, of course, but that kind of courage and intestinal fortitude and willingness to pursue a goal are very much needed. Call it aggressiveness or whatever, humans in combat situations need that trait as well. Both canines and humans need to have those drives and traits, but the key, obviously, is not just to possess them in over-the-top quantities but to be able to harness them and use them in appropriate situations in appropriate ways.

It is also important to understand that when I acquire a dog from a breeder of Malinois, I'm not getting a very young puppy who hasn't been trained at all. The two-to-three-year-old dogs have already gone through rigorous training; some even have become what is referred to as a "titled dog." That means that they've been trained and have earned a certification in one of several different European dog sports. One of the more common types of those is Schutzhund, a dog sport popular in Germany. When this sport was first organized and the competitions formalized, a dog that had completed Schutzhund training and became certified in the sport was also essentially qualified to be a German police dog. That was the original intent of the program, but between politics and hurt feelings, the dogs that earn the "title" don't necessarily have the competency to become actual working police dogs. The sport is so popular that other breeds of dogs now can enter into the competitions.

Similar to what I've described previously, these competitions test to determine to what degree these dogs possess traits such as courage, intelligence, perseverance, and protective instinct. There are three levels of achievement, and the tests cover three aspects of the dog's abilities—tracking, obedience, and protection. A dog must pass all three phases of the test in order to be titled. In addition to the Schutzhund, there are Belgian Ring, French Ring, Mondio Ring, and Dutch KNPV, as well as other organizations and titles with some minor and other major differences. The distinctions among those groups and titles aren't as important as this basic point: the dogs we acquire must all have the necessary traits and instincts that are essential and required to do the type of demanding job we are going to ask them to do.

Typically, these dogs will have some obedience, "bite work," controlled bite work—where the dog has to "out" or release on command. It will have completed an article search/tracking exercise in which the dog has to go through numerous obstacles and then find a person or an object. While this all sounds good in theory, and it does have its benefits, a problem arises because each trainer has his or her own way of doing things. We may come back with five titled dogs, but because each trainer uses different methods and even words for commands (not just a different language), such as the English equivalent of saying "here," "come," or "get over here" to get a dog to come, we then have to do things our way. There are some exceptions to that, of course, and most of our dogs still know the language they were first taught in, and most often we continue to use that language.

In a sense, this is like what the navy used to do with its prospective SEAL Team members. It would first put them through basic training and then require that they study to achieve some rate (job title) even before going into BUD/S training. For example, I had to go through four months of training as an intelligence specialist and then went to BUD/S. Recently the navy has changed its policy and made being a SEAL a rate in itself, meaning you can join the navy and go straight to BUD/S right out of boot camp. That level of preparedness is oftentimes minimal, but no one goes into a SEAL Team training pipeline or deployment as a human or canine without it. We all come from different backgrounds, have had different experiences, and that has an impact on how we learn and what we learn, just as it is with the dogs. We can't create exact duplicates of humans or canines, and as a trainer of SEALs and their dogs, I can tell you that wouldn't be desirable or possible. We have a template in mind, but we always have to make allowances for the individual personality and skills those warriors possess. How much allowance is made varies, but the most important consideration is that dogs and men live up to the high standards set for both of them.

4

No matter how well bred a dog is and how well done the initial training is, we are still left with a lot of work to do before a dog and his handler are ready to be deployed. That is also true of the individuals who volunteer to be dog handlers. I've spent a lot of time training both the handlers and the dogs, sometimes separately and sometimes together. Even though someone is a great SEAL Team member, that doesn't mean that he will function well as a handler. Just because a dog has earned his title, that doesn't mean that he'll be a great SOF dog.

That's just the nature, and the nurture, of the situation. I say this because, obviously, when we're talking animal and human nature, both of those influences come into play. In this chapter, I'm going to talk mostly about the nurture side of the equation. I also want to make it clear that while I travel overseas to source dogs for use with the SEAL Teams, I'm there as a buyer and not as an observer of the training methods those Dutch breeders employ. (While I've sourced dogs from other places, I generally get them from Dutch breeders.) I talk with them a bit about how they conduct those initial phases of instruction, but my primary goal when I travel there is to acquire dogs, generally ones that are about two years old or more, and not to acquire any additional information about how to train dogs to do detection and apprehension work.

That's not intended to be a slight against those owners/ breeders. The fact that their dogs are the ones we end up with speaks volumes about what they're capable of doing. Once we get those dogs to the United States and begin our more focused phases of training to prepare them for the work they have to do specifically with the SEAL Teams, we have a lot more than just a head start. We've got canines that are extremely capable and intelligent animals with a very good foundation for adding to their repertoire of skills. This analogy may fall somewhat short, but it's as if we get these dogs with a high school education: they've graduated with honors, and we next put them through college and graduate school. As our program advances, the skills we focus on narrow to a point of high specialization, much like a human would in earning an advanced degree.

Before I get into that sector of training, I want to spend some time talking about what those first couple of years might be like for those dogs we acquire. To do that, I'm drawing from my own experience working with dogs born and bred right here, many of which go on to work with a variety of governmental agencies in various capacities. While what I do from the time a pup is born until it is ready for its advanced education may differ in some respects from what the SEAL Team dogs go through in their first few days, weeks, and months in Europe, for all practical purposes, those differences in methodology are almost immaterial. We are attempting to do the same thing: maximize the natural abilities of the dogs, identify their areas of strength and weakness, and expose them to as many different environmental stimuli as possible so that they can more easily adapt to the specific circumstances they will encounter in their "careers."

Again, that comparison between the human members of the SEAL Teams and their canine co-workers applies. No one goes into the SEAL Teams without first completing basic training and then one additional level before starting BUD/S training. While there is a 75 percent attrition rate among those entering BUD/S, we don't have that great a failure rate among the dogs. I haven't kept statistics to track that rate among the dogs we acquire, but it is more like three or four in ten instead of seven and a half out of ten.

Part of the reason for that is that the early weeding-out process among the dogs is more vigorous than it is among the sailors. As I stated earlier, I felt the first test I had to pass to qualify as a SEAL Team candidate wasn't very hard at all. When I'm evaluating prospective team dogs, my standards are much higher. In addition, when we select sires and bitches for breeding, we already have in mind the kinds of work that these dogs will be asked to do. As a consequence, we breed for those qualities, and from the moment those dogs are born—to be more precise, in the first several days of their lives—I'm already beginning their training. Even before that, I've tried to optimize their chances of success by providing their mothers with the most stress-free environment possible during their gestation period. Generally, that means moving them to a different kennel area. I place them as far as possible from the clamor—mostly other dogs on the premises. This limits the possible stress produced by other dogs' barking and limits their contact with overly aggressive or rambunctious trainees on the premises. At any one time, I may have as many as a dozen to two dozen dogs around, including my house pets, so you can imagine the level of noise these dogs can produce. That's especially true because of the kennel I've built for them.

I've built a kennel run that has indoor/outdoor climate control. It's all cinder block, epoxy coated, with a full-on septic system with heavy-duty drains and everything. While that provides a cool and sturdy structure for them to live in and allows them to be in or out of the weather, the indoor acoustics don't provide the most peaceful environment. I've come to learn that unstressed bitches produce the highest-quality litters, so I make accommodations for the mothers even before they whelp.

All dog trainers have their own theories, and some of them are scientific based. A lot of them are old wives' tales or just the experiences that they have had that seem to work the best for them. I've done a lot of training and seen a lot of good and bad results. And I can tell you that the methods that I'm about to go over are the ones on which I've seen empirical data backed up with studies. I've also seen the good results from them, and I've seen bad results from not adhering to these principles.

Basically what it boils down to is that the puppies are a kind of blank slate, but they absolutely retain some of their pack-animal instincts. That said, they are also domesticated to the point where they can go either way—resort to some of their human-aggression tendencies or adapt to life with people. If they have very little human interaction in the first couple of months of life, they're going to be polar opposites than if they have had a ton of human interaction.

From day 3 to day 21, we do what's called "biosensor stressing," which sounds a lot more complicated than it is. Biosensor stressing is simply this: it's messing around playfully with the puppy. But there's a structured routine that we put them through in that first couple of weeks. When you pick the dog up, you want to do a couple of things. One, you want to tickle its feet. Usually I'll take a Q-tip and stick it between his pads and his toes, basically making sure to stimulate each one of his paws. Doing this gets them used to being handled by humans and in a way desensitizes them to the kind of probing that's a necessary part of maintaining and assessing their health and ability to work. Along with that, I'll hold him completely upright, in other words, with his head directly above his tail. I'll place him up next to my face to let him smell me. I'll breathe hot breath on him, and I'll talk to him.

In those first few days, dogs' sight and their hearing are not fully developed. So early on, neither my smell nor my physical presence is as fully recognizable to them as it will eventually be, but I want them to have that early sensory experience as soon as possible. That way, as they're developing those senses more fully, they'll have that early experience of what I smell like, what I sound like, and what I look like already in place. I want them to be comfortable with me. I also have multiple people do it so that the dogs get exposure to as many people as possible to establish that comfort level with humans. At a minimum, I want adult males and adult females and several different children to be around these puppies, but I bring many people around them. As you can probably figure out, it's not hard to get people to hold and play with puppies.

Besides that first phase of tickling the dog's feet, I hold him upright, hold him upside down, hold him on his back, and then put him belly down on a cold, wet washcloth for just a couple of seconds. Then I put him back in with the group and grab the next one out, and do that with every one of them. I'll usually do that routine in the morning and at night. And then throughout the day also, I'll constantly be picking them up and just kind of playing with them, holding them—like I said, putting them up next to me against my face, letting them smell me, see me. As they progress, that human input will be valuable.

I also start to play CDs of random noises. Several different companies make noise CDs that are typically used to expose police horses to various auditory stimuli. Essentially, they are antispooking noise CDs. They have train engine noises, whistles, firecrackers, thunder, machine guns, different farm animals making noises, creaky doors opening, cars driving by, mufflers backfiring, engine sounds, sirens, honking, and so on. Imagine any big city's soundscape, and that's what's recorded; I play it back repeatedly. Again, this is all about getting the dog accustomed to what is a very large part of their environment—sound. Dogs have sensitive hearing, and our selective breeding of them has enhanced that ability over their other canid relatives (wolves). Also, because of the structure of their ears, they can hear sounds coming from a greater distance. Pointed, erect ears are most effective at capturing sound waves. I've read claims that a dog can hear sounds coming from a distance four times greater than the distance from which a human being can hear. These mentions don't cite the specifics of the studies or how they were conducted, what breed of dogs were used, or the like. As a result I'm dubious at best about quantifying a dog's superiority in terms of the distances over which it can detect sound waves. That's not really one of the detection scenarios we train for.

I've seen more credible studies that put a dog's audible sound range from 40 Hz to 60 kHz. Humans, by comparison, have an audibility range of 20 Hz to 20 kHz. What that means is that dogs can hear sounds of a higher frequency than we can.

Obviously, a dog's hearing is an asset on the field. However, if we were to select a working animal to detect sound, and we did that solely on the basis of the animals with the most acute hearing, we'd probably want a rabbit or a gerbil. I've read studies, again reported with less than ideal accuracy about the methodology, that claim that those animals and others have far superior hearing than even dogs do. They wouldn't be as effective in the field for a lot of other reasons, and our technology has advanced to the point where devices do that kind of work incredibly well. Also, you wouldn't want to put up with the kind of teasing and jokes you'd have to endure with your working rabbit.

The point of our exposing the pups to these different sounds isn't to improve their auditory acuity; it's just to get them to not be startled by new and strange sounds. Anyone who has had a dog can attest to the fact that certain sounds, like the whine of a vacuum cleaner's motor, can really irritate a dog. We don't want to overstress the pups, but we do have to get them accustomed to hearing a variety of noises and at various volumes. Later, when we do helicopter training with the candidates, that early exposure almost always pays off. All you can ever do in training is simulate how the real world of their working lives will be; how they respond in those real world instances is never a certainty. Training is all about enhancing the likelihood of a good outcome down the road.

At about the time the pups are weaned (at four weeks), I'll stop using those noise CDs and shift into another phase of their early training. At that point, I begin to work with them on evaluating and enhancing their prey drive. To do that, I'll take a rag, like a dishcloth or terry towel, and tease them with it. I want them to get their eyes focused on it so they will chase it. I tease them a little bit, then they chase, chase, chase. *Bam*—I reward them by letting them get it. We play a little bit of tug, and then I reward them by letting them have the rag. They're tearing their prey off, basically.

One of the other things I do is wean the dogs very early. Some people will wait until they're seven or eight weeks old to start getting them off the mom. I get them off the mom as soon as possible for two reasons: (1) it's a lot easier on her; (2) I want to be present to teach them some manners while still allowing them to get some of their mannerisms and character from the mother. I also want a lot of human interaction at that point. I'll go into this concept in far greater detail in talking about the advanced phases of their training, but the single most important aspect of a dog's training for the work they do is to establish a bond of trust between handler and dog. That begins in those early days with getting the dogs accustomed to human contact.

Why is this so important? Even among animal behaviorists, and among trainers and breeders, there is some disagreement about the extent or even existence of the pack mentality. It's beyond the scope of this book to get into this in any great detail. Based on my observation, I would say that, yes, to an extent dogs do possess this instinct. However, it is something that is easily overcome, and there are likely very few dogs that are aggressive, or more aggressive, when around other dogs. There are many more components that make up a dog's aggression toward humans than just simply to say, "That's their nature."

I will say this: if they're left with littermates, a litter the size of eight, for example, and they have no human interaction, they're going to be very, very pack oriented, or very, very animal dependent. On the flip side, dogs raised this way are going to be much weaker when they're isolated. So I try to get them by themselves with me, with other humans, solo humans, as early as possible, because that's the environment they're going to be in for the rest of their lives. They're going to be paired up with a human, they're going to be in kennels and crates and in different environments doing all these exercises. So I ingrain in them that this is the standard, this is the routine from day 1, and then they don't know anything else. We don't ever want them to be thrown off too much by being in a new situation that may cause them to get confused or to lock up.

The same is true with human beings: new environments and stimuli can cause us to not perform at our peak. The navy has long realized this, and that's why training exercises are so important. The closer the simulation can be to the real thing, the better prepared you're going to be when immersed in the real-world situation. That point may be obvious, and for all the work a pilot or tank commander may do in a simulation, or the more times a soldier uses a sophisticated kind of video game, the more comfortable they will be in an actual scenario. Nothing beats the real deal, but short of that, simulations work with dogs and humans.

Of course, the first time you attempt something, whether you're a dog or a human, things can get a little bit ragged. The notion of practice makes perfect is definitely true with the dogs we prepare. It's also equally true that the first time we do anything new with the dogs, we see the pointy end of the learning curve—and sometimes that pointy end can pierce you.

Because of the nature of the work that SEAL Teams frequently engage in, being comfortable and beyond competent in the water is a must for human members of the team. The same is therefore true of the dogs. Most of the dogs that we get have had some "exposure" to the water. That term can mean a lot of things—from drinking it to actively swimming in it. Like most of the training they receive before they come to us, those experiences aren't the most positive reward-based training exercises they have. As a result, we have to do a lot of reward-based work with them to get them comfortable with swimming. Like most things we teach or learn, we start out small and basic and advance from there. We toss a ball into the water and let the dogs chase it, tossing it farther and farther over time, so that those first few opportunities in the water are equivalent to wading before we get into the high-pawing/paddling/splashing technique that some of them employ early on.

Eventually, after many repetitions and rewards, we get to the point where the dogs have to go out on what I call conditioning swims along with their handlers. Obviously, as SEALs, these guys are quite capable in the water, and the dogs have definitely developed a "near to the beach" comfort level. At this point, we stretch them out in the ocean, or in Balboa Bay or elsewhere, to the point where they can no longer see the shoreline.

Once, when we went out on a group conditioning swim, the handlers and dogs were in a loose pack with the dogs on a modified type of lead. We were all headed on an out-and-back swim beyond a buoy. The dogs and handlers were all doing well past the first five hundred yards or so. I was with them, and I saw one of the dogs, Luke, get a look in his eyes that I'd seen before.

The dogs are smart and have great instincts for self-preservation. They are all not just looking ahead and around at the other dogs and the handlers, but they're taking a peek back to their origin point. Well, Luke took a glance back, and all he could see was water. When he turned his face back toward me, I could see the panic in his eyes and his face. Pretty soon, that panicked looked turned into a sodden expression of anger. Luke took off after my partner in training, Wayne, and it was clear he was bent on destroying someone or something. It was as if that dog had decided that if he was going down, he was taking someone with him.

Also, in Luke's mind—and I've seen this in dozens of other dogs that weren't quite so aggressive or pissed off about it—he viewed anything bobbing in the water along with him as a bit of land he could find safety on. For about fifteen minutes, I thought I was in the middle of *Jaws 1D*—1 dog. Wayne did his best to fend off that dog, flanking him while Luke turned tight circles, his paws like a razor-sharp paddle wheel, his bared teeth like white shark fins. Every time Luke got close, Wayne would push Luke's hindquarters away from him. When he couldn't get to his flanks, Wayne had to resort to pushing at Luke's neck and the side of his head. It was quite a battle, and the rest of us, as you might expect, got quite a laugh out of Wayne's struggles

I'd been in that position myself, not with a dog as bite-aggressive as Luke, but with dogs that were so scared, the rate of their paddling and their desire to climb on top of you to get up out of water combined to potentially turn you into human cole slaw, and it had you at wit's end. The thing that Wayne couldn't do, and none of the trainee handlers could do in this situation or in any other, was to give in and let the dog have its way. If you did, you had a major problem on your hands. That dog would then rise thirty places in his mind on the mental totem pole that signified his status. Cave into a dog like one of these once, and your life could be hell. As it was, many of us ended up getting parts of our bodies raked by the thumbs and dewclaws of a panicked swimming dog, and those raised welts became just another way that we all earned our stripes.

Far better to endure that pain on the so-called practice field than in a real game. The price we'd pay in lives lost if a dog panicked during a swimming insertion was not something I wanted to think about, but it was certainly something I wanted to prevent. As tiresome and frustrating as it might have been to do that kind of work with the dogs, in an environment that is relatively foreign to them, it made me realize just how important patience and follow-through were in doing this kind of training. It also reminded me of a mission I participated in, and how the right preparation can make all the difference.

In the run-up to Operation Iraqi Freedom in early 2003, I participated in a bit of navy history. As a part of our general maritime exercises (you can even go to the SEAL's Web site to see photos of these drills), we climb up to an oil/gas platform's superstructure from a NSW rigid-hull inflatable boat (RHIB) piloted by Special Warfare Combatant-Craft Crewmen (SWCC). We did those types of exercises often, but when we knew that an upcoming mission would involve this kind of work, it took on a new sense of urgency.

Six weeks prior to the onset of the ground warfare, we learned that we were tasked with taking over two oil terminals in the Persian Gulf. This was going to be my first big mission. Because of the sanctions and embargoes levied against the Iraqi regime, these two oil terminals had taken on strategic importance. They were a bit dilapidated, but because of where they were, the Iraqis had used them increasingly to smuggle oil out of the country. Supertankers would berth there and then sneak out again loaded with crude. The two forty-eight-inch pipelines that ran along the floor of the gulf were pumping millions of barrels of oil, and the fear was that the regime, anticipating that they were soon to be invaded, would blow those pipelines, preventing the allies from using that oil and also creating a huge environmental disaster and distraction. They'd also make us look like the bad guys and blame us for the resulting explosions, fire, and oil spill.

We also had had some intel at the time that said that the platforms were rigged with explosives and that they were going to be blown up as soon as we got on board. At one point we heard that there were more than a hundred Iraqi Republican Guard troops stationed on the rigs and that they were going to stand and take their death fighting us if we came and tried to take over the rigs.

So it was pretty harrowing because we had thirty-two guys in a couple of small RHIBs that we were going to ride in on to assault this target. So if the intel was correct, we were pretty badly outnumbered, and they had the platforms rigged to explode.

Even without knowing all of that, we would have taken our training seriously, but we took it up a notch. We built an exact replica of those platforms, which were separated by several miles of open water, by the way, and practiced and practiced a coordinated assault on them both, along with on a metering station and pipeline manifold many miles away from those two rigs. We had three big targets to neutralize at the same time. We figured that if there was any slipup in the timing, one or the other of the locations would have a communications system in place to notify the others to detonate the explosives placed at all three.

So, I was taking part in the largest operation in the history of Naval Special Warfare. All of SEAL Team 3, all eight SEAL platoons, were assigned to take down these targets simultaneously. To put it mildly, this was a huge logistical nightmare. If we pulled it off, that would be spectacular. If we somehow didn't, it could be a spectacular disaster.

The platforms were enormous, sixteen hundred meters (approximately one mile) long, with a berthing station at one end and smaller substations running the length of each one—all potential places where the Iraqi soldiers could be hiding out. We knew the rigs were manned, but didn't know the exact numbers. I can't tell you the number of times we rehearsed that operation, but dogs and men both learn by repetition, and overrepetition doesn't exist. We had multiple scenarios, including the use of two helicopters to aid the assault, and the list of what-ifs and what-to-dos in case those what-ifs occurred became my waking and sleeping reality.

By the time we set out in our heavily armed Mark V boats—their superior firepower and cruising speed made the journey from the Kuwaiti Naval Base to the point at which we transferred to the RHIBs in two hours—I was dry mouthed and the pucker factor was high, but I was also ready; our training couldn't have been any more thorough. I still remember looking over at our embedded journalist, Steve Centanni of Fox News, who had accompanied us on the Mark Vs, and wondering what the hell he was thinking—how did he get in on this?

By the time we transferred to the RHIBs, I no longer cared what he was thinking; I had a job to do. My one last, stray thought as I looked out across the gulf's waters to the winking lights of the Iraqi mainland was, *Holy shit, I'm one of among thirty-two guys who are kicking this whole freaking thing off.* If that can't get you excited, you're a dead man.

Ultimately, we found twenty-three Iraqi soldiers on board, a mixed bag of Republican Guard and Fedayeen Saddam guys. We also captured a few Iraqi intelligence officers and a couple of their navy divers. We struck in the middle of the night and took them totally by surprise. They never got to use the explosives or the antiaircraft artillery (AAA) piece that was positioned to take out approaching watercraft. We basically caught them completely off guard. We discovered a treasure trove of weaponry and ammo, but with our element of surprise, we captured them all without a single casualty on our side. I was one of the main breachers, using a shotgun to open about thirty metal doors to begin clearing each of the areas. In total, it took six hours to take the whole thing down, including prisoner handling and doing initial interrogations.

The same was true at the second platform. At the metering station, the resistance was even stronger, and a few Iraqi soldiers were killed, but again, not a single American casualty, wound, or injury. That's a pretty raging success in my book, and I was and remain pretty damn proud of being part of SEAL Team 3's role in setting the tone for what was to come. We didn't have long to celebrate. As soon as we got back to the Kuwait Naval Base (KNB), we packed up and headed to the Ali Al Salem Air Base. And in that couple of days, that's when the ground war started. Once again, we were on the move to a different environment, working in places very far from the waters of the gulf, but we'd been prepared for those conditions as well.

Since that night, and given what I do today, I've often

wondered how multi-purpose canines might have helped us. Certainly the mission was a resounding success, but we'd placed many troops in great peril, which we all understand is part of the deal, but how might dogs have made our jobs a bit easier?

Having gone through that experience, when I made the transition to training SEALs and later to training dogs to assist them, that mission played a large role in my motivation and in my understanding of the importance of the work I was doing. I wanted the dogs I trained to be able to meet those high standards of effort and execution that were exhibited that night. I was going to be sure that the dogs I trained were ready for anything, anywhere.

Again, because adaptability to an environment is so key to their success, I do a couple of other things to enhance both prey drive and the pups' comfort with the unfamiliar. Even at a young age I start taking them all over the place, to the local hospital, playgrounds, to Home Depot—you name it. Since these dogs will get transported to various locations a lot during training and afterward, getting them used to being in a vehicle is essential. We go into parking lots and let a lot of people handle them and play with them and see them. We also want to expose them to people in different circumstances and environments—people in wheelchairs, on crutches, kids in shopping carts; we take the pups on escalators, elevators, through loud noises, into dark rooms, and onto slippery floors. As soon as I can get these dogs exposed to stuff like that, I do it.

I also do the rag work in all these different types of environments. I'll basically set up a little puppy obstacle course, where they've got all different sorts of objects and obstacles to deal with—lengths of PVC pipe lying on the ground, little baby pools with plastic bottles in them, a suspension bridge that's elevated and unstable, fence grading, or single-level and multileveled pallets. I want them to have to crawl up and over things, go underground at times, and be familiar and comfortable in all kinds of terrain. One of my favorite sights is seeing the dogs dive into that kiddy pool filled with empty plastic bottles in pursuit of a ball or a toy. Later, when the pups get bigger, I do this on a larger scale with an old bathtub filled with plastic balls. If you've ever taken your kids to an inside playground and seen them in that pit of balls, you can imagine what these dogs are like. Except, none of them, or a very rare few, will pause on the edge, thinking about it before diving in.

I really enjoy working with the pups at all stages, but I get a big kick out of building what is essentially a doggy Disneyland for them and watching them figure out all the rides. That doesn't mean that my interaction with them is limited to me watching. At this stage, I'm very much into hands-on play with them. I do a lot of throwing with mini tennis balls and toys. I also still do a lot of rag work and tug-of-war, with tug balls attached to a string to keep them in pursuit of something as much as possible. I really want these dogs to develop their sense of possession—that there's something out there that they have to get, and once they do, it belongs to them. Later on, we'll work more intently on the letting-go part, but first, really feeding their desire to chase takes precedence over that.

To reinforce the idea that these other locations are pleasurable and offer some kind of reward, I will also feed them. Like any breed, the Malinois we use differ in their food drives; regardless, any reward experience they have that pairs the place with the meeting of a need offers positive reinforcement. But I'll also start to feed them and start to get them using their noses early on, too. I'll take a bowl of food and set it somewhere in the whelping room. Not right in the middle of it, but somewhere they have to search a bit to find. You'll very quickly see them smell the food, and they'll starting using their noses and they'll go find it. After a few days of that, I put it in the training room, somewhere just beyond the whelping-room door. Now they come out into the training room. Same thing: it's already preplaced somewhere, they get wind of it, they all use their noses, all follow and find that bowl of food.

Every couple of days I'll up the ante, so to speak, and make it more challenging for them. We'll go outside. Now training is in a field, and they've got twenty-five to thirty square meters to search. And I'll set them up for success. I'll put them down very near where I hide the food, because their attention span is incredibly short for approximately the first twelve months. So I'll do that outside, and then I'll put it in the deep weeds even farther away. Then I'll hide it several acres away, and they'll just start walking. Again, it's important to understand that I don't want to frustrate them too much, just enough for them to earn their taste of success. So, when I go outside to hide their meal, I'm always going to place it somewhere downwind. That way, when they first step outside, the odor cone—how the molecules travel from the source and out and away from it—presents that food to them pretty quickly. As soon as those pups catch a whiff of it, they go charging out after it.

I've worked at multiple things by doing it this way. First, I've taught them to use their noses and to be successful. They have gotten proven results, and several repetitions of being successful using their noses at an early age also helps teach them, frankly, to just use it and trust it.

But they've also had to do some work. When we're out in larger and larger areas, they have to stick with it and keep air scenting and walking along with me. We walk and we walk, and then, *bam,* all of a sudden we're in odor and we're going to source locating and finding. This is exactly what they're going to be doing in detection work later on.

It may sound like I'm being pretty demanding on these pups at an early age, and I am. But I'm not punishing them in any way, and in a lot of respects, as serious as this business is, the dogs are also having fun. No, you wouldn't train your kids this way, but these are dogs being trained to be working dogs. No dog has ever starved or been injured in any way during this early training phase. That said, I want them to learn to work for a reward from an early age. I know ahead of time what their role in life is going to be, the kinds of skills they are going to use to be successful. If you look at any person who is successful at a sport, the chances are that they began *playing* (note the emphasis here) at a very early age. The best athletes are generally the ones who picked up the game very early. Sure, you could become a pro golfer, tennis player, baseball player, or whatever if you started at the age of fifteen. But the odds are against you. The earlier you get a start, the better your chances of being at the top of your sport someday.

When doing detection work, a dog will take as many as ten short breaths a second to get those scents far into their nasal cavity. That early work in having them cover larger and larger amounts of territory is just a prelude to the kind of endurance and detection work they will do later on.

If I haven't convinced you yet that these dogs are extraordinarily capable, imagine a human covering the distances these dogs do, kilometers at a time, while employing that kind of breathing pattern. We'd likely faint before we'd finish. While dogs, particularly herding dogs, have strong endurance capacities inherently, that natural trait also has to be carefully nurtured. Eventually, these dogs will travel great distances on walks, sometimes carrying weighted vests; other times they will do resistance training against Bungee-type elasticized cords while walking on treadmills, and other work to heighten their athletic abilities.

Nature has given these dogs a leg up, maybe two; nurture—the training methods we use—helps them get all four legs up on the competition. The successful intertwining of both nature and nurture produces the best results. I use the expression "You can only polish a turd so much" when talking about this issue. The combination of a great genetic background and solid training produces the dogs that work with the SEAL Teams. There are no shortcuts in either nature or nurture. Both take hard work on the part of man and canine, though I believe that the dogs actually enjoy doing the training work. They get to exhibit the traits that their breeds were refined to produce, to give expression to both their innate and externally reinforced natures. What can be better than that?

Those genetics have to be maximized in order for a dog to reach its potential.

When I take a step back and consider what these dogs are doing in the environments they are doing them in, it truly blows my mind. And this is why those dogs can do the things they do: it's because of people who are meticulous about breeding, who are meticulous about raising, who are meticulous about training. They absolutely bust their asses in every facet of everything that has to do with these dogs and leave nothing to chance.

I make my living and stake my reputation on training dogs. As a result, my livelihood depends on doing things the best way possible. Also, as a former SEAL Team member, I take very seriously the responsibility that these dogs and handlers shoulder. I couldn't live with myself if I knew that I didn't do everything in my power to make certain that the dogs I provide live up to the standards expected of SEAL Team dogs. Lives depend on that.

It helps to know that, as a vendor, my dogs are going to be rigorously tested; when the men who purchase the dogs from me for use with the SEAL Teams or any other agency come to test my dogs, they're going to throw everything *and* the kitchen sink at my dogs to make sure that they are what they need. And if there is a single hole in one of these dogs, they're going to find it. And so you have to set these dogs up for success or they're not going to be the best. I never heard my parents say, "That's good enough." I wasn't raised that way; and the SEALs didn't train me to think that way, either. The SEAL operators deserve, as they say, "Nothing but the best for the best."

— 5 —

In the previous chapter, I spent a lot of time talking about what we do with pups to begin the training process. As I said, and I hope it is abundantly clear, for the dogs and for me, this is more like fun than anything resembling work. One additional component of making it fun and working with these dogs, rather than dominating them, is that we also offer these dogs abundant praise when they do things right—find the ball in the tub of bottles, get to the food dish, or whatever. Praise is essential to getting these dogs, or any dog for that matter, to do the things we want them to do. It's also important to note that the praise can come verbally or nonverbally and preferably both ways—with words and actions.

I don't know about you, but I've heard parents say this more than a few times to their children (and it was said to me on a few occasions): "It's not *what* you said, it's *how* you said it." That is so true for dogs. The nonverbal component of the language we employ with dogs is far more important than the words we use. Dogs learn through repetition and simple association. If you wanted to, you could teach your dog to lie down by using the words "get up." Dogs don't understand the meaning of words; they simply associate the words we use, through repetition and reward, with an action or an object. For example, if your dog was used to you calling a stuffed animal with a squeaker inside a "toy," and then you placed a plastic scale-model dump truck in front of him or her and told her to get the toy, chances are she wouldn't retrieve that truck. The plastic item might fit within the classification we humans have made for toys, but the dog wouldn't make that same association immediately. Over time, if you did enough repetitions with the dog and rewarded it for picking up that plastic truck, your dog would make the association between the sounds you make to form the word "toy" and that object. It would know that the stuffed animal and the truck belong to the same category of things. Unless that category is things I can put in my mouth—which for dogs encompasses a whole lot of their universe.

What's my point? Dogs are essentially nonverbal animals. They respond to sounds that we use as words, but they react more to intonation—volume and pitch—much more so than the words. Anyone who has had a dog will tell you that if they use an excited tone, the dog responds better and in kind. If you yell and sound angry, the dog will respond to the emotional tone of your voice and to a lesser degree the words themselves. "Bad" and "no" have no real meaning unto themselves to a dog; it's the associated or corresponding actions and nonverbal components of the utterances that they really understand.

This may be a fine point of distinction, but it's an important one in several contexts. I often tell people that the only language dogs know is body language. That's a bit of a stretch because of what I've said about intonation above, but dogs primarily read posture and other nonverbal cues we give off. They are highly, highly sensitive to the "vibes" we and other animals, and in particular other dogs, give off. They also "speak" nonverbal/postural language among themselves.

You've probably encountered this situation. You're walking with your dog on or off leash, and you encounter another dog. The sniffing process begins. Have you ever noticed how one dog will place his head near or above the other dog's neck and shoulders? What does the other dog do? It stands up taller and holds itself rigid; its ears either lie flat or more likely stand up. That dog is sending a clear message by making itself appear larger, as if to say, *You're not going to mess with me.* Sometimes the dog will make itself appear smaller: it will shrink itself, lower its hind legs, lie its ears back flat, and generally assume a very passive posture. It's communicating with its body.

I frequently use this analogy when talking about our interactions with dogs. Many times people come by my place, where I have a few retired military working dogs. The people are often interested in adopting them and caring for them. I make sure they understand very clearly the specific characteristics of working dogs and how they may differ from pets. I've seen people bend down and want to enter the dog's crate or kennel to greet the dog. I immediately stop them and tell them to imagine this scenario from a different perspective: You're in a ten-by-ten prison cell. Someone comes into it to join you. They're bigger than you are, they are making some sounds you don't understand, and they want to wrap their arms around you like you're old buddies or something. What are you going to do? How are you going to respond, especially if you're a type-A person?

My other point here is that dogs understand body language and they understand the environment they are in. That whole fight-or-flight instinct comes into play in this scenario. They've got no place to go, you've backed them into a corner, so don't be surprised if they come out fighting.

Another reason I talk about this is that I equate some of the old-school establish dominance/become the alpha male or pack leader training approaches to this kind of nonthinking approach to training. As I pointed out before, the key to working with a dog is to establish a bond of trust between you and him. I do that with puppies from the very beginning, and you can also do that with dogs you acquire at later stages in their lives. Since dogs learn by association, I want them to associate me with all good things in their lives: the food they eat, the water they drink, the things they play with, the exercise they receive, and on and on. One simple thing I do to establish that bond and their association with me as a source of positive things is to feed them and give them water. I may take it away from them briefly, not to tease them, but to get them to be understand through repetition that *Hey, this guy is the one who gives me what I want.*

How does this associative learning work, and what are some of its limitations? For example, your dog observes you reaching into your pocket to retrieve a treat. You then present that treat to the dog. He understands that something good comes from you reaching into your pocket. Through enough repetitions of that action, or of you holding a ball and him associating being able to play with it, those associations get hardwired into their brains. If you reach in your pocket and pull out a set of keys, or you hold an apple or an orange in your hand, your dog is going to make the same association as before—*I'm getting a treat* or *I'm going to play*. Only when you allow it to see and to sniff those other objects, and repeatedly not reward it after these same actions, will it figure out the difference.

Studies have been conducted to compare the relative intelligence of dogs to humans, and the estimates are that an adult dog has the smarts of a four-year-old human. I'd have to disagree a bit with that and put the range at a four-to-seven-year-old human. Even though I've said that dogs learn by repetition and association, they do have problem-solving skills. For example, I've had dogs that have watched me open the latch to a gate enough times that they've then figured out how to open it for themselves. As you'll see in the stories of the dogs in action, they are capable of carrying out a series of complex and long-duration tasks independently.

Oddly, I see some advantages in the limitations of associative learning. Maybe it's just me, but sometimes the complexities of human interactions grow frustrating. Raising kids is an example of that. At the ages of four to seven—that span of years that encompasses the intellectual capabilities of dogs—you spend a whole lot of time *reasoning* with a child. You can engage in seemingly endless conversations about whether a behavior, an utterance, an impulse, or a thought is right or wrong. With dogs, you don't. They are far more black and white in their view of the world, and the kind of operant conditioning and associative learning they do works very much to your advantage. *A reward means I did something "good," so I should keep doing that so I keep getting rewarded.* Anyone with a child will tell you that children will test that equation six ways to Sunday—*If I do this, will I still be good? If I do that, will I still get rewarded?*

That's not to say that dogs should be automatons that simply factor in stimulus and response. They should still be somewhat freethinking. I use a clicker during training to mark behaviors—a simple kind of association tool that allows me to communicate to the dog that the behavior it just exhibited was a proper/acceptable one. In the beginning, I hold a treat in my hand. I sit there looking at the dog, he looks at me, I click, and then he gets the treat. Naturally, the dog will start to offer up behaviors, hoping that one of them will get me to reward him. I don't even have to give him a command, and I don't. If he goes into full down position, I click and reward. If I want to teach him to bark on command, I wait until he barks, and then I click and reward.

As another example, if I want to get a dog to go into his crate, I place a crate in the middle of a clear room—one with no other distractions; if the dog takes a step toward that crate, I click and reward it. If he takes another step, I repeat the process, and so on. When we get to more complicated tasks, that same process applies. With the crate, repeat that often enough, and the dog will go in that room, see the crate, dash into it, lie down, and wait for the treat/reward. This is a win-win situation. The dog gets a treat, and I get the desired outcome.

Obviously, I could put a prong collar on a dog, give no treats, and I could get to the same place by punishing him for not doing what I wanted. He will learn just as quickly what the answer is, but there's an enormous paradigm shift between the positive and the negative. You've got a dog that is doing what he's "supposed" to do because he doesn't want his ass kicked, versus a dog that is doing the right thing because he wants to, because he wants that reward. One builds trust, the other destroys it.

What's important to remember is that that kind of training is, in a sense, an act of coercion—getting an animal to do what we want it to do, not letting it do what it naturally wants to do. The other side of the training coin, one that isn't a win-win, and one that I don't like to see used, is the old spiked/pronged/electric-shock choke-collar approach. I mean that literally and figuratively. A spiked training collar, a whip, a stick, or any other tool to mete out punishment to show a dog who's boss, to punish it when it doesn't do what we want, may eventually get a dog to do what you want, but at a great cost to the dog. So why do it?

You can use one of four methods of operant conditioning to train a dog. The first is positive reinforcement. Keep in mind that the word "positive" in this case refers to addition—giving something. The classic example of this is a rat in a maze receiving a reward, a food pellet, when it successfully reaches the end of the maze. The opposite of that is, obviously, negative reinforcement. Here, "negative" refers to taking something away, or subtracting. Again, using the rat-in-the-maze experiment, if a loud noise is made while the rat moves through the passages, and then it is silenced when the rat succeeds, you've used negative reinforcement—you took something away but still rewarded the rat by getting rid of that awful sound.

The third type of operant conditioning is positive punishment: you add a stimulus, usually something painful, when a behavior you don't want occurs. An electric-shock collar is an example of that kind of operant conditioning. Negative punishment, as you can probably guess, is taking something away when an undesired behavior occurs. Your kid acts up, so you take away her cell phone.

For 90 to 95 percent of the time, when training dogs—either pups or adolescents in early or advanced training stages—I use positive reinforcement. I equate relying heavily on the other three to this: you want your kid to learn algebra, so you set a book down in front of her and demand that she does the equations starting on page one. You don't provide any kind of instruction or encouragement. You only use positive punishment or negative punishment as consequences. She can't solve the first problem, so you slap her hand. Repeat and repeat. Sure, at some point your kid might learn algebra, but it will take a hell of a lot longer and be more painful for you and for her if you do it that way. Far too many trainers and handlers spend far too much time using positive and negative punishment. They may get results, but the essential bond of trust between a trainer and a dog won't exist. A dog may do what you want out of fear or to avoid pain, but that kind of relationship is one that will always be out of balance. Just like the Navy SEALs are a team and watch out for one another in every way because of their trust and respect for one another, the same has to be true of how a military working dog and his handler operate.

Another takeaway from that algebra analogy is that you almost always have to go into a situation when training a dog carrying along this assumption: they don't know anything but body language and the environment. They are not stupid, they are not incapable of learning, but they do need to be taught. Invariably, because dogs learn through association and repetition, the learning process will be longer than we might like. For example, once dogs enter into our advanced training, even though they're already titled, it may take one to two years before they are ready to be deployed. That's a lot of time and innumerable repetitions before they are truly ready to do the important work necessary of them.

Besides my respect and love of dogs and the value we place on the human/canine bond, I spend so much time using positive reinforcement simply because I can't imagine how hellacious my day would be if I spent the vast majority of it punishing the dogs. How awful would that be? I can't imagine the toll that would take on you mentally, and it's no wonder that I see people, both in the military-working-dog community and pet owners, allowing their emotions to get the better of them. One of the most frequent mistakes I see people make with their dogs is that when "correcting" them, they get the dog to either stop doing what they didn't want it to do or get it to do the thing they wanted, and they continue to either berate or punish their dog. That's incredibly confusing for a dog. *You told me to stop, I stopped, and now you're still screaming at me or correcting me. Does that mean that you don't want me to do what I'm now doing?*

With pets, you end up with dogs that aren't clear about what's expected of them. That's not good. With working dogs, when excessive punishment is used, you end up with either a handler-aggressive dog or a broken dog—not in body but certainly in spirit. We need dogs with intense spirits to take on the challenges of being outstanding detection and apprehension dogs. As I've pointed out before, the pool of suitable dogs is relatively small. To see a dog with the right characteristics ruined by poor training methods is both heartbreaking and an enormous waste of a valuable resource.

Negative and positive punishment can break the spirit of a dog and this is especially true of dogs that are just entering adulthood, the prime age for specialized training. It seems counterintuitive to me that we select and breed dogs to have a fierce and courageous demeanor and then try to take that spirit away from them, especially since they will need that kind of character to charge into the austere environments that we ask them to. With the dogs we train, we want and need them to feel like they are kings of the world. They better have a nasty, hard, confident attitude, since they may very well be taking on insurgents who want nothing more than to kill them and their human associates. They've got to have a pair on them that will allow them to charge through the gates of hell to go bite a guy who's not going to just sit there and let them take him down.

So, if you've taught a dog from the age of seven weeks on that he's below humans in the chain of command, and he's then going to do whatever he's told out of a desire to avoid pain, whenever the pressure of a human being is being placed on him, he's going to fold. I don't care how strong a dog is genetically, if he's been trained in that dominated/coercive/ negative way, he's going to be ruined. He's learned through his whole life that a human being can dominate him. Would you want to go into battle thinking that? Whether it's a friendly game of tennis, softball, or whatever, if you go into it thinking you can be beat, chances are you will.

That's not to say that there doesn't come a point in a military working dog's training when the dog is old enough, powerful enough, that you as trainer have to set some rules and teach the dog certain manners and obedience, or you're going to end up losing fingers or getting puncture wounds all up and down your arms. That kind of uncontrolled and naked dog aggression is counterproductive as well. Simply put, though: if you are counting on a dog to work to protect you, to apprehend human bad guys, they can't be scared of anyone.

Sometimes the demands of the marketplace mean that a dog is rushed through the training pipeline too quickly. Some trainers make too many demands too soon on a dog after they first acquire him. Since there's a demand for dogs to do all kinds of work for the military and other governmental agencies, there's obviously a temptation to rush through the process. Using negative reinforcement may seem like one of those ways to get a dog to market sooner, but in the long run, I've seen that backfire. The same is true of not fully understanding some of the developmental stages that a dog goes through. Raising dogs and raising children are similar in some ways, but there are a couple of crucial differences. From birth to eighteen months, a dog goes through a rapid period of mental and physical growth, from helpless "infant" to an animal possessing the vast majority of its adult capabilities. With kids, recent studies have shown that they don't reach full mental maturity until much later than we thought—into their mid-to-late twenties. Those are two very different time frames.

The window of opportunity that you have with a dog is much smaller, obviously, but that's where the patience has to come in. Getting a dog and immediately thrusting it too soon into the kinds of specialized training we do can overwhelm it. Letting the dog acclimate to a new environment is essential.

Keep in mind that environment is so critical in training and in the field when these dogs are deployed. Exposure to various environments, and not just climate or topography, but indoors, outdoors, on stairs, in helicopters, on narrow walkways, in the dark, and so on, is something that I spend a lot of time on when I'm preparing pups for training. It's not something I want to have to do when I acquire a candidate dog for SEAL training. That's not to say that any good trainer couldn't take an eighteen-month-old dog, or older, and eventually get the dog to be comfortable in those various environments, but it would take an awful damn long time to get to that point. And, as I stated above, you just don't have that kind of time. That's why I spend so much time with pups getting them over whatever apprehension they might have about unknown/strange environments. They have to associate overcoming that fear with something positive—a reward. Some of that is genetic, what we call the nerve of the dog, but dogs can also learn to set their fears aside. Both aspects—genetics and training—are required to be successful.

Detection work is very complicated, and as a result, the

training has to be very segmented and very regimented. I'd say that there are as many as two hundred steps to doing it well, and as we progress through them, if we encounter any snags along the way, we'll fall back a few steps and then work forward and hopefully past that problem area. Dogs will then have performed some of these exercises and discrete tasks with thousands of repetitions before being deployed. Because they learn through association and repetition, consistency is the key to training working dogs or pets. Anyone who owns a dog knows that his or her dog likes routine. It isn't so much that they like it; it's how they live their lives.

That's why training is so time-consuming. I have to be consistent in how I approach every task. When working with dogs on their detection work, that means that I have to get a dog from his crate, get him to sit, go down on one knee, hold the dog by the back of the collar, show him the ball, rub it against his chest, and then feint a throw to let him know that it is now time for him for go to work seeking an object. All those things I did prior to that were kind of like priming the pump, letting the dog know that a reward—playing with the ball—is going to follow soon.

As a trainer, you also want to watch the response of the dogs to the anticipated bit of play that is to follow. Early on, when you're not wanting to do much of anything to deter his enthusiasm, you get used to the idea that you're holding a ball, and involuntarily you begin to blink, and by the time your eyelid has completed its trip, a sixty-five-pound dog has launched itself with all four paws from a standing start to your eye level, with his jaws snapping in anticipation and un-controlled glee. I'll get to how these dogs respond when they get to do their favorite training—bite work—in a bit, but these multi-function dogs spend the majority of their time detecting odors while working in the field. Because of the demands of being able to detect multiple odors, a large part of their specialized training time is spent on this skill.

The object of this training is to take full advantage of a dog's innate ability to detect odors far better than a human can. The estimates vary, but a frequently cited estimation of their superiority over us claims that a dog's sense of smell is a thousand times more sensitive than that of humans. Part of the reason for this is that dogs have more than 220 million olfactory receptors in their noses, while humans have only 5 million.[1] In 1999, researchers at Auburn University's Institute for Biological Detection Systems conducted experiments to determine how those canine receptors work and at what threshold (in parts per million) of an odor a dog can still detect a specific odor when a target odor is intermixed with other odors. Their intent, essentially, was to determine how little of a substance needs to be present before a dog can no longer detect it. According to their report, "The dog's limit of detection (absolute threshold) has been determined for four compounds to date. These sensitivities are in the tens of parts per billion (ppb) for methyl benzoate, cyclohexanone, and nitroglycerin. The sensitivity to DMNB, a detection taggant, is much greater at 500 parts per trillion (ppt). There is no reason to believe that these thresholds are not representative of thresholds for other compounds."[2] In other words, the dogs could detect these explosive compounds when only 10 million or so parts per billion were present. They could also detect another substance that is used in the making of explosive compounds (a detection taggant), which many governments, including our own, require be placed there as tags or identifiers to "label" the active ingredients of the explosive. These taggants are volatile chemicals that are released into the air and are designed to essentially "serialize" certain compounds our government wants to keep track of. Because they are designed to be detected, those taggants can be present in even smaller quantities (500 parts per trillion) than the chemicals that make up the actual explosive.

Okay, that's the science lesson for the day. The important thing to remember is that we're talking about really, really, really small quantities of those chemicals being present in order for a dog to detect them. When you get into the difference between millions and billions, you know that you're talking about, in this case, incredibly small quantities.

That Auburn study also went on to talk about the need to not train dogs in terms of the weight of the explosives being hidden for them to detect. What's important is that the chemicals give off molecules of odor and that the farther the dog is from that hidden cache, the fewer of those molecules are available. Because of their keen sensitivity, they will hit on that small number of molecules and then move toward the area of greatest concentration—the explosives themselves. That's pretty common sense, but we use that notion of the odor cone all the time in creating detection scenarios. More on that in a bit.

The main question is, How do you train a dog to detect anything? Exposure (or association) and repetition come into play again here. This time, though, you don't need thousands of repetitions. In my experience, exposing a dog to a specific chemical signature for, let's say, TNT, to get them to recognize it and become familiar with it and to be able to detect that specific scent only takes a handful of times.

Think of it this way: how many times did you have to be exposed to skunk odor before you could positively identify that smell?

To do this kind of initial detection exposure, trainers use lots of methods, but I employ one that I refer to simply as retrieving. We don't want dogs to randomly detect any odor, obviously, so we have to get the dogs to respond to specific odors/chemical signatures. Most of those chemical signatures we want them to detect are for substances which they normally wouldn't encounter and haven't encountered at any time in their lives prior to their training.

The obvious point about odor detection is that you have to introduce the dogs to that chemical signature somehow. The medium you use to expose the dog to that odor is essentially irrelevant. You can enclose it in a PVC pipe with holes drilled in it, boxes, towels, or anything else that will retain that small bit of the explosive material. I use rags, bits of terry-cloth towel, but I'm extremely careful with how I use them—not because they could explode, but because they can become easily contaminated. I wear latex or nitrile gloves whenever I'm handling the samples to avoid my odor signature from getting mixed in with the explosive material. I'll place a small amount (several pounds) of explosive in a plastic box along with a quantity of towels. After about a month, the explosive odor has worked its way into the fabric. At that point, I can then separate the towels and seal them individually in an airtight container (think Tupperware) and label it.

Early in the exposure regimen to imprint an odor, I won't be too concerned about the environment in which I do the work. That will come later. I first take a dog out, along with his handler, and we work on the simplest level. I throw the towel, and the dog retrieves it. His reward, when he brings the rag back to his handler, is that he gets to play tug for a little bit with the towel. We repeat those retrievals fifteen or so times, and by the end, the dog is familiar with that odor. I use a new towel each time to make certain that the dog is fixed on that odor and not the combination of dirt, grass, spit, the handler's odor, or anything else. It takes the dog about ten minutes to become imprinted on the odor, far less time than it takes me to do all the prep work.

After the imprinting, we move on to what's called point-to-point exercises. For this, I need a fenced-off area; ball fields work really well. I take a sample of that odor and put it on the back side and upwind side of the fence; I may place half a pound of a selected target odor there. I then take the dog, or have the handler take his dog, and I give the search command. Then I walk alongside that fence so that we are parallel to the chain link, downwind and in a straight line. Depending upon how hard the wind is blowing, we may start out walking toward the dynamite from only about fifteen feet away. The wind blowing across that dynamite creates the odor cone. It starts out narrow at the source and then widens; picture a flashlight beam's spread.

As we're walking and entering that odor cone, I'm watching the dog to see any change in behavior. When he hits on the odor, his head will snap in the direction of the odor, his tail will feather or twitch, and his body will move in the direction of the source. He'll get up to the fence but not actually be able to touch the explosive, lick it, eat it, or whatever. At that point, I train the dogs to either sit or lie down as the means for the dog to alert the handler, "Here it is." The dog does either of those two actions, I hit the clicker, and then the dog gets his reward.

We work through that scenario one odor at a time, over and over, until we move through all the possible detection scenarios for all the desired target odors we want to teach them to recognize. Another advantage I have as a former SEAL is that I understand and have experience with the tactical side of explosives. I can create more realistic scenarios for the dogs to work in than someone who is a dog trainer first and an explosive-detection dog trainer second. I was trained as a SEAL, I was deployed as a SEAL, I've trained SEAL Team members, and now I use all that to train military working dogs to assist SEAL Teams. Having been there and done all that means that I can be as precise as possible, giving these incredibly talented animals the benefit of my experience.

To get a dog to detect anything, basically you'd follow those same fundamental principles of initial exposure/imprinting, point-to-point, and then various environmental scenarios. In order for dogs to endure those environmental scenarios, they have to be in top physical shape. They go on runs and swims, and run/swim/runs with their handlers. They'll do resistance training with either weights, dragging weights attached to a harness, or with Bungee-cord leashes, which, the farther they are extended, the greater the resistance produced.

Apprehension work incorporates a bit of detection work; the dogs search for human odor, but it is primarily about one thing—bite work. When a handler wants his dog to go out and do detection work, the most frequently used command is *"sook,"* what our Dutch breeders told us means " search," "seek," or "find" an object. The dogs get very excited when they hear that. They go positively nuts when the handler tells them *"reviere,"* which instructs the dog to find a human. That command also lets them know that they are going to be able to do what is probably their favorite thing of all—bite someone.

That is as harsh as it sounds, and until you've seen these dogs do their bite-work exercises, I don't think you can really understand the relish these dogs bring to this task. I pointed out early on that these dogs are bred to be alpha males, top-of-the-heap, aggressive types, and nothing brings that out in them like the opportunity to sink their teeth into something or someone.

Someone recently told me the story of their Labrador retriever mix chasing and catching a deer fawn. The dog, who weighs about seventy pounds, is probably more active than most pets, very fit, but hardly an aggressive dog. The owner suspects that on a 10-point scale, the adult male is a 4 or a 5—neutral, in the sense that it never shows aggression toward humans or other dogs but doesn't cower or retreat completely when approached by other canines. The owner wasn't surprised to see the dog chase the three adult deer and the single fawn. However, when it caught the fawn, dragged it down from the rear, and then grabbed it by the neck and hoisted it off the ground, he was surprised. The fawn was about the same size as the dog, but the power of the dog's neck and jaw muscles that enabled it to lift and shake the fawn wasn't something the owner expected to see. He ordered the dog to stop, and it did, and the fawn, its heart racing and its legs wobbly but with no visible wounds, ambled off into the woods to join the adults.

I share this story because it highlights the fact that dogs and their prey drive, which to this point we've mostly talked about in terms of chasing balls, is an impressive sight. The speed with which dogs chase their prey, the strength they possess, and the instinctive move to shake their prey to snap its neck is present to a certain degree in nearly all dogs. The Labrador retriever mix in question here had killed a few voles and a lone squirrel prior to that incident and had chased its fair share of deer, fox, and, unadvisedly, a couple of elk prior to that fawn. It had some of the drive and tenacity of the Malinois we use, but certainly not to the same degree. The only reason it was able to catch the fawn was that its prey tried to hide behind a pile of fallen trees. The only reason the fawn survived was that the dog's jaws were not powerful enough to puncture its skin, couldn't whip it with enough force to break its neck, and it was willing to release its prey easily on command.

In a similar scenario with one of our military working dogs, the outcome for the fawn would have been very different. Most likely the fawn wouldn't have had the chance to go into the kind of defensive hiding position, and that initial grab/ bite/shake would have likely been lethal. When a dog that is a 10+ on that prey drive/aggression scale goes into action, he generally gets what he's after and concludes the matter swiftly. That's not to say that these dogs don't need to work on their ability to attack and subdue human targets; they very definitely need to have their fighting skills refined.

I need to make this point clear from the start. The apprehension work that we do with a dog is to train it as a non-lethal force. Just because these dogs would have killed the fawn in that scenario above is not to say that they are trained to do the same thing in their work as SOF dogs. In most cases, a live capture of a suspected or clearly demonstrated insurgent, Taliban member, or other bad guy is much preferred over a neutralized one. A lot of valuable intelligence has been extracted from captured combatants. That is one of the reasons why I consider a dog to be such an effective weapon: it is a very highly skilled nonlethal force.

In some ways, calling what we do in this regard "bite work" is a bit of misnomer. Yes, we do teach the dogs some things they need to know, but as I pointed out in the previous chapter, when they are given the command *reviere*, to find a human, they do so with a desire that goes beyond a mere *Ho-hum, here we go again, I've got work to do* approach. As I mentioned, the difference in their demeanor when instructed to do detection work for explosives and when told to find a human target is substantial. They are eager in both cases, but there's a palpable sense of the dog's own explosive capabilities when on the hunt for a bad guy. It is as if every cell in the dog's body, every bit of its canine ancestry, and the accumulated learning and experience in being able to provide for itself are turned on.

Having put on a bite suit or sleeve myself and felt the power of these dogs' bodies and jaws, I can tell you it's not something to take lightly, and I would not want to be on the receiving end of those blows and bites without that protective gear. In fact, I have been, and it's an incredibly humbling experience. Even when wearing protective gear, I have at times experienced a level of pain as intense as anything I've endured.

As is true with exact measurements of a dog's aural, olfactory, and vision capabilities, accurate measurements of a dog's bite force are difficult to come by due to the variables involved. In those cases when a laboratory setting and testing procedure has been set up, those measurements also are questionable. For example, one study of canine bite force, conducted at the University of Guelph in Ontario, Canada, used a protocol during which the dogs were anesthetized and had their jaw muscles stimulated electrically. My sense of this study, and others in which dogs bite down on objects with sensors attached to measure the bite force, is that they don't account for the adrenaline rush that would naturally occur in a more "natural" setting. We've all heard stories of what people are capable of lifting when faced with an extreme situation, and when a dog is anesthetized or placed in a clinical environment, I don't believe that its emotional and physiological response would be the same as it would be in actual (or practiced) combat.

Nevertheless, those measurements do help establish some kind of baseline data. For example, in the Guelph study, a German shepherd was able to produce a bite force of 170 pounds per square inch at the front of its jaw and 568 pounds at the rear. Common sense will tell you that the rear number should be higher, since that's closer to the lever point. Those numbers are impressive, but fall far short of the claims that I've heard of a dog being able to exert up to 2,000 pounds of pressure. As Stanley Coren pointed out in his May 2010 article "Dog Bite Force: Myths, Misinterpretations and Realities" in *Psychology Today,* that 2,000-pound figure (which would be roughly equivalent to a subcompact car being parked on your radius bone or ulna in your forearm) is likely the result of people not paying close enough attention to the units of measurement being cited. A 2,000-newton force is roughly equivalent to 450 pounds, since one newton is approximately a fifth of a pound. That puts us closer to the Guelph-study measurements.

Recently, Dr. Brady Barr, in a National Geographic television series entitled "Dangerous Encounters" and first broadcast in August of 2005, conducted similar kinds of live bite tests with a variety of species. He equipped a bite sleeve with a computerized measuring instrument and found that his human test subjects reached 127 pounds of pressure, while domestic dogs averaged 320 pounds. In comparison, lions and white sharks reached 600 pounds, while hyenas exerted 1,000 pounds, and crocodiles 2,500. That's an impressive figure for the crocodile, but apparently Dr. Barr wasn't satisfied with that performance, believing that the croc was just messing around. He redid the test and the croc rose to the challenge, reaching 6,000 pounds.

The scientists conducting the Guelph study published their results in Volume 214, Issue 3, of the March 2009 edition of the *Journal of Anatomy*, but it was for a second type of test they performed. For this, they used the skulls of dead dogs, took various measurements, and applied complicated formulas to arrive at some conclusions about how the size and shape of a cranium and jaw can affect the amount of pressure a dog can exert. They used terms like "cranial morphology" and "phylogentic analyses," and lever formulas like $CBF_1 = (Lm \times M = Lt \times T)$ FPA/O_c to develop their evidence. Their detailed analyses came up with a conclusion most of us would have suspected: larger dogs exert greater bite force, and larger brachycephalic dogs (those with a proportionate lower jaw but a shortened upper jaw) have an advantage over mesaticephalic dogs. Dogs of this latter type, the most common skull shape, have a cranium portion that is roughly equal in size to the nasal cavity. In other words, the head of one of these dogs is roughly divided into equal portions of what we think of as the skull and the snout.

Malinois are mesaticephalic in terms of skull shape and are a large breed. According to the Guelph study, the statistical mean, or average, bite force for dogs with these characteristics, depending upon the level formula used, ranged from 2,749 N, or 617 pounds of force, to 2450 N, or 550 pounds at the molar, and between 170 and 150 pounds at the canine teeth at the front of the jaw.

That's a lot of numbers and scientific jargon, but it does have real-world implications. Obviously, a dog clamping down on you with the front of its jaws isn't going to exert nearly as much force as a dog that clamps on and then chomps forward, getting you with those back teeth. If you've ever observed your dog as you played tug with them, it becomes apparent pretty quickly that the dogs understand something about the physics of bite force, and they work pretty hard to get whatever they've got between their teeth into the backs of their mouths to hold it more securely. If you've ever attempted to pull a tennis ball out of your dog's mouth, you know that it's easier if you get it at the front and not the back.

It's also pretty obvious that a dog will first bite with the front of the mouth; after all, that's the widest opening and it makes access easiest. You can go on the Internet and see videos of protection dogs and other working dogs doing bite work, and you'll see some pretty spectacular flashing of jaws and snarling and men in bite suits getting these dogs to grab and hold on with those front-of-jaw bites. Looks great, but if you've learned the physics lessons from above, those bites won't exert as much force as back-of-the-jaw clamping. Those canine teeth are sharp and will puncture skin, but when it comes to bone-crushing power and the ability to really hold on to and subdue an adversary, a dog will have to get those back teeth on you.

Similarly, you can also see amazing scenes of flying dogs going after trainers in bite suits. These dogs launch themselves from twenty feet away and then contact their targets. Looks great. Not very effective. As any football coach will tell you, don't leave your feet. Why?

As a former football player I can tell you that it's hard to change direction in midair. As a dog trainer who's been in various apprehension/bite-training scenarios, you can't change direction very easily when your feet are off the ground, and it's a hell of a lot easier to feint left or right and avoid a charging dog that doesn't have four (or two) paws planted solidly. In addition, the amount of force and leverage you lose when you're airborne versus solidly planted on the planet is substantial. In the NFL, some of those soaring tackles make the highlights reel, but the ones when the defensive player is firmly planted on the ground and drives the ball carrier back are not just more fundamentally sound but also inflict far greater punishment.

Also, those leaps are dangerous to the dog's well-being. We want the dogs to recognize what environment they are in. If they take off after someone who is on a roof and the dog leaps, generally, they have a predictable path of travel while in the air. If they take off from twenty feet away, that gives the bad guy more time to move out of the way. Depending upon the locale, the dog could sail off that roof, hit a wall, or otherwise do serious damage to itself.

Essentially, then, when we teach dogs in bite-work scenarios, the techniques that we want them to develop are these: stay low and planted, continue to drive forward, and, to a lesser extent, get those back teeth involved. The reason why the last of those three is of lesser importance is that the dog's natural instinct is to do that. The front-teeth grab is easier for the dog, and when they have you in that lesser-pressure grip, you can inflict some damage on them. That means that we have to work with the dogs to get them to be relentless, to continue to stay on the offensive despite the punishment they're receiving, so that they can get that back-of-the-mouth crushing pressure on you.

Let me tell you, all those studies aside, I know that when a dog gets that maximum bite force on me, it is incredible. The pain is sharp and intense, my vision narrows, sounds seem to be silenced, and thoughts of how I can mess with this dog and get the better of him are replaced by a single thought: *I wish this dog would get the fuck off of me!*

Bite work is always a tricky thing, and even more so when working with a younger, less-experienced, or less-trained dog. When you factor in some of the other things I've mentioned about building plausible training scenarios and exposing dogs to various stimuli and environments, that bite-work-danger level rises. Once again, I've got to use Matt and Arras as an example of how events can sometimes get out of hand. We were on a training mission at night again, and Matt was wearing his Night Observation Devices (NODs) when we were in the mountains. By this time, he and Arras had done other night exercises, but this time we were introducing a new element—gunfire. We stress with the handlers the importance of taking that quick moment to really think through options before acting—as Matt was painfully aware after tumbling down that hill after a ball reward went bad.

Terrain, the dog's temperament, and many other factors play into having simple control over the dog. There's also the tactical side to consider. We use the mountains frequently and at night especially because those two things combine to produce about the most difficult environment the handlers will encounter. As they grow more confident and competent, we have to up the ante. The dogs and handlers will be going into tactically complex scenarios, and that means that they have to be prepared to deal with the possibility of enemy contact and engagement. That means weapons.

By the time we introduce nighttime gunfire into a mountain exercise, the dogs have already been exposed to the sound of weapons being fired. Essentially, they've been hardwired through breeding and training to have an aggressive response to the sound of a weapon's discharge. To prepare them early on, we have a man in a bite suit fire a weapon and then flee. The dogs, of course, are supposed to pursue and subdue that individual. That's seldom a problem for these dogs. They associate the sound of gunfire with aggression. That's both good and bad. Due to the types of operations the dogs engage in, an immediate aggressive response to gunfire is not tactically sound. Consequently, we have to get them to not respond to gunfire, to desensitize them to the sound, and to only go into apprehension mode on command. The only way to do that is to fire round after round near them, reward them when they don't freak out, and restrain them when they do.

During this night-training gunfire exercise, Matt and Arras

were out on a patrol scenario. One of the "decoys"—a trainer in a bite suit—crossed their path and fired off a couple of rounds. Matt did as he should and gave Arras the command, and the dog pile-drove the decoy to the ground, subdued him after a few minutes, and then heard the out command that Matt issued. This time, instead of returning to Matt's side calmly, Arras, who was still very green, turned and looked at Matt, face clad in his NODs equipment and also carrying a gun, and took after Matt, leaping up to bite his handler in the middle of the chest. He drove Matt to the ground and had him in a very vulnerable position when, thankfully, he better recognized through scent and other inputs that this was the guy who was taking good care of him, and he immediately released Matt.

In a fast-moving, dark, and chaotic scene like that, it's easy to understand why Arras responded that way. It's also easy to understand why we were all so grateful that Arras didn't utilize his full capabilities as a biter. Anyone involved in the training of these dogs has to have, or will quickly develop, respect for the potential threat that these dogs pose.

Another new environment for dogs is around and on a helicopter. We do a similar kind of exposure work with them, working from just having them be around the aircraft, to getting into one, to actually taking off and landing, and then flying in one over a greater distance. We refer to those takeoff and landing exercises as "doing elevators." We place one dog in each helicopter along with a compliment of a crew and a team. The dog and handler are the last to board. We do the full load-up, dog and handler get on. We take off and then land two to three minutes later, repeating this process six to eight times with the dog.

Everyone knows that the dogs just starting out with this training can be a bit apprehensive, and I've watched as backs press to the chopper's fuselage and eyes go wide as the handler and the dog board. Once, we had a relatively inexperienced flier doing elevators. The others in the cabin were all handlers, so they knew what to look for, and they all watched the dog and immediately wall-papered themselves. They could see the dog defaulting to aggression mode, and he eyed every one of them, assessing who would be the choicest bite. The men kept pressing themselves against the cabin wall, each one trying to make himself as small a target as possible. I had to laugh a bit when I saw that. Five combat-trained and hardened frogmen, heavily armed, mind you, trying to keep as far as they could from this pacing menace. Obviously, we have to get the dogs to calm down and not pose such a threat, but those exercises serve as a good reminder to all of us of the kind of power these dogs have over us and how we have to do everything we can to harness it and unleash it properly.

I think it bears repeating that you can't get a dog to get over that revert-to-aggression mode by doing anything punitive to them. You would further incite that response and thus have to be even more punitive to the point of absolutely breaking the dog's spirit. What we do is make those frightening and unfamiliar experiences more pleasant through the use of rewards. In training, even in bite work or getting a dog used to a muzzle or anything else, I carry with me some treats. Toys and food rewards work most often, and when I'm working, I carry both. I even take soft treats and mash them against the inside of a muzzle cage to get dogs that are unwilling to put their snouts in there to get them to associate the muzzle with a positive. At first, just letting them eat treats out of the muzzle is an effective way to get them used to the sight of the apparatus. When it comes time to place the muzzle over the dog's head and snout, it's much easier if they aren't already on high alert or anxiety at the sight of the thing.

No matter what you're trying to do with the dogs to train them for the role they will play in combat or in your life, it's important that they believe that some positive reward is coming their way. As trainers and handlers, our positive reward system also provides us with a growing confidence that we won't be the ones the dogs turn their considerable bite force on.

All those numbers in regard to bite force pale in comparison to something that's difficult to quantify—the measure of a dog's heart and how much abuse it's willing to endure in order to subdue a human being. They've all got that potential to exert upward of 600 pounds of bite force, but how many of them are willing to do it at the expense of their own discomfort? That's what the bite work in a contained area is all about. Think about it like this: we work on developing their tenacity in close combat, similar to the way a boxer spars in the ring. We're also working to develop their technique, but it's also about getting them to utilize their inherent aggression and push past a pain boundary—some physical pain, but mostly mental stress. When a dog feels you fighting back, when it feels your mental and emotional aggression working against its forces, that you are really locked in combat, then you are really testing the dog's willingness to get the job done.

Working in a bite suit against a dog is as much an acting job as it is a physical performance. Similar to what the dogs have to endure, more than just your physical stamina is being tested. As I said, dogs speak body language and pick up the energetic projections you give off. If you are working with a dog on its apprehension and bite skills, you have to be mentally strong and able to project the same kind of *I'm bigger and badder and more willing to beat your ass than you are mine* attitude. Anyone can go through the motions of standing there in a padded suit while a dog grabs him; it takes a good bit of artistry to act the part (and, believe me, it isn't completely acting) of someone who has deadly intent. Dogs are highly sensitive to those signals we humans send out, and they absolutely get it when we're afraid, and they take full advantage of it. It's how they respond when you match aggression for aggression that determines whether or not they make the cut with us.

Just to give you a sense of how strongly dogs respond to those signals we send, I have a close friend who can give off such a fierce vibe that he can be on the ground, a very compromising position, and when we release a dog to come after him, it will tear out initially and then come skidding to a stop six feet in front of him, sensing that he is one badass dude and thinking, *I'd better be careful.* My friend doesn't shout, doesn't strike other offensive postures, he just exudes a *don't mess with me* mentality that the dogs can feel. Similarly, in some videos you'll see a decoy flailing around, yelling and screaming, but the dogs aren't focused on those vocalizations or actions. That looks good on the camera, but the dog isn't really seeing or hearing that at all; in fact, the dog is more focused on prey movement and reward than what the decoy thinks he is projecting.

The way that we get dogs to match aggression for aggression is by transferring between drives. When you're doing apprehension or bite work, there are two main drives that the dog is working. He's working in prey drive and he's working in defensive drive. In my opinion, it should be offense and defense, just for congruency and for simplicity, because I honestly believe prey drive is all offensive. Identifying when a dog is in prey drive is pretty much learned from or derived from rules in nature or in captivity. Animal behaviorists and also trainers study how dogs react, observe their body posturing, see how a dog fits within its pack structure, and then make educated guesses about why the dogs do the things they do when pursuing but primarily confronting another animal. When an animal makes a choice to fight a human, it is an offensive decision. The key words here are "makes a choice."

In bite work, a dog starts out in prey drive (offense), and that's very instinctual. He sees a guy in a suit, he gets the command, and, *bam,* he goes after him. He's conditioned to fight with the guy. What usually doesn't happen in most of the dog sports, and in much of the other bite-work training other dogs receive, is that they aren't truly put into defense. I equate that to a boxer who's been taught how to box but has never been hit. So you've got to teach this dog how to get hit, how to react. You can take anybody and teach him how to throw punches all night long, how to move around the ring, to counterpunch. But if he's never actually been hit, the first time he gets hit, he'll be, like, *Holy shit, what was that?* And so you've got to teach that dog that *Hey, not only is it okay, but you're going to work through it.*

And so it's a very, very simple, but not an easy process. You've got to have a truckload of experience of seeing dogs being worked, and then also working them to really identify and transition through these two drives. Prey relieves their stress. They feel like this is the natural order of things. *I'm being the aggressor. I'm taking it to that thing. I'm going to dominate it.*

So when in prey drive, the dog detects something, his mouth is on it, he's biting down, he's scoring the touchdown. He's getting after it; he's loving life. And then all of a sudden, the decoy (the person in the bite suit) comes alive and starts bringing it to him. *Now I'm going to fight. Now I'm going on defense. Now I'm getting a little bit worried about this guy. I'm fighting him a little harder, maybe going a third round.* You've got to be able to recognize when the dog is in prey and when the dog is in defense. Put the dog too much on the defensive and for too long, and it will crack. We damn sure can't have that happen.

To keep the dog on the aggressive, we gradually increase those defensive thresholds by transferring back and forth between prey drive and defensive drive: *I'm going after it; I'm preserving my life.* Over time, that threshold for defense goes up and up and up enough to where that dog is automatically coming at you like he wants to kill you. And it doesn't matter what you do to him, he is completely unfazed by it. It may start out with the dog in prey, so you put a little bit of pressure on the dog and he starts to kind of wig out a little bit. *Bam*—you switch right back into prey and relieve that stress. Now you go back into defense. Now he lasts a few seconds longer, he starts to show stress, and—*bam*. Every time he starts to get to that boiling point—*bam*—you go right back into prey. I back off, I reward him, I look away from him, I let him dominate me, and I take a bite to the back. Maybe I fall to the ground and let him really dominate me.

You're constantly evaluating this feeling-out process. A truly good decoy is someone who is absolutely priceless because he will make or break a dog. You can ruin a great dog with a incompetent decoy, or make an average dog fantastic by having a phenomenal decoy who can recognize those times of transitions and know how much pressure to put on, when to back off, when to relieve stress, when to put it on.

In my mind, doing this kind of bite work is absolutely an art. The science of animal behaviorism is absolutely behind it, but putting that fundamental understanding of a dog's assertive nature into practice to refine those instinctive skills isn't something you can get from reading a book. You need to see a really, really good decoy who can work a dog and put him through that and imitate some of those behaviors. That will get you to a certain point, but you also have to eventually develop a feel for how stressed a dog is, recognize its body language and how it is communicating what it is thinking and feeling, before you can really train a dog well. You elevate this dog to a level where you, again, are teaching him how to fight, how to bring that natural instinct he has genetically deep down, which we're already identified through our selection process, and now we've just teaching him to bring it at a much higher level to be able to take the rigors of the training. And it gets to where he's ten times the dog that he was when we first got him.

Like other things involved in training military working dogs, it's a time-consuming process. If you're not careful, you can create a couple of problems. One is that if you don't put enough defense on the dog, then he never really, truly learns how to fight. This is certainly better than burning him out going the other way, which is putting too much defense on him. Now you've cracked and ruined the dog, and now his spirit is broken, and he relinquishes a lot of the backbone that he had. As a result, we always err on the side of prey drive and not taking the dogs overboard into the defensive.

Unless you've seen these dogs in action, it's difficult to convey the differences in their responses when in each of the two drives. It is a matter of degree of intensity as well as specific behaviors. In terms of intensity, think of your dog when you reward him with a treat: he takes it readily and willingly but is gentle and nonaggressive. When you give your dog a treat and other dogs are present, your dog's sense of competition for resources is higher. He will take the treat, reaching for it more aggressively, and, in some cases, turn his head and his eyes seem to roll back, in the same way that a great white shark does when attacking prey. Your dog won't bite you in order to get the treat, but he definitely is amped up a notch or two. That's how it is when military working dogs transition from one drive to the other. Because the intensity is already well beyond your treat-seeking dog's drive, their amped-up behaviors feel that much more aggressive/assertive.

The other component of apprehension work is placing the dogs in a variety of environments, just like we do with detection training. A dog that will only fight when in a kind of training corral isn't any good to us. Neither is a dog that is distracted by other stimuli. As a result, we travel far and wide and create a variety of topographical and situational scenarios so that the dogs have experience tracking and apprehending bad guys in everything from mountainous terrain to urban settings, both indoors and outdoors.

So, how do we refine the dogs' innate skills to make them effective at apprehending individuals? Just as with the detection work, we start them early, we continually increase the complexity and duration of the exercises—moving from play as pups to more serious work as adults—and push them to near their breaking point.

Beginning in the four-to-five-week time frame, we start to develop and encourage that prey instinct. We always take advantage of the dog's inherent desire to want to chase moving objects. So we'll take a terry-cloth towel or a rag, something that's very easy for the dog to grip, but something you can tease it easily with, and we'll develop that prey instinct so that it becomes a useful skill for things other than just playing tug-of-war.

As you've probably experienced if you've ever raised a pup, when you wave something in front of it, it's going to chase that thing and try to grab it. In our work, we do something similar, but with the intent of getting them a little bit frustrated that we have a hold of it. You tug with them a little bit, and then usually when they bite in a little bit deeper, we give them counterpressure by pulling back a little bit and holding still. The dog will usually naturally pull a little bit and then counter and go a little deeper. When he does that, I'll let go of it and reward him by letting him have the towel or rag. It's as if I'm saying, *Okay, you chased it, caught it, killed it; now you get to carry your prey off and prance around, and it's yours, and you get to have it, have fun.*

From that, we advance to doing that work in all different types of environments. We do it in buildings, out in fields, dark places, vehicles, or anywhere else that they may or may not encounter in their later training or downrange. And so the dogs are not just environmentally going places; they're chasing balls in those environments, they're doing rag and bite work in those environments.

And just like every other step of dog training, as time progresses, we very slowly baby-step forward. From rags we'll go to a puppy sleeve, which is basically just like a jute pillow. It's very soft; it's very easy for the dogs to grab on to. The same principles apply to what we did with the rags and towels.

Sometimes we'll take a twenty-ounce plastic bottle and flatten it and tie it to a string—making a "flirt pole"—and tease the dog with that because it's a much different material. It's very hard to hold on to. That teaches the dog that if he wants it, he's going to have to bite down hard and hang on hard or he's going to lose it. With cloths and rags and the puppy sleeve, the dogs can kind of half-ass the grip and still hang on to it because they've got sharp little puppy teeth that dig in and hold on. That doesn't work on those plastic bottles.

Even at five or six weeks old, when they're grabbing a rag, we pick them up off the ground, raising the back end higher than the mouth. We pat them hard on the rib cage. We place them on a slippery, elevated surface, still doing the bite work with them. Basically, we are just teaching them that no matter what position their bodies are in, no matter what environment they're in, that they're going to be okay and they just need to keep those jaws clamping down.

From there, as the dogs age to the three-, four-, five-, six-month phase, during every couple of training sessions we increase the intensity in some way. One day we may increase pressure that we're putting on the dogs. We'll increase the hardness of the sleeves and the biting material, the thickness, judging what they can take. But it's a very, very slow process.

Once the dogs have their adult teeth in completely and they're fully set, usually around seven to eight months, then we'll start to get into the bite suits and introduce those elements and start to teach multi-area targeting. To do that, as the dogs are coming in, we don't stand the same way or offer the same body parts to them every time. That's not realistic for "street dogs" or ones like the SOF dogs that aren't going to be doing this in a competitive environment. For sport work, where accuracy and the ability to target a specific area is measured and scored, that's fine. Our dogs will be fighting people in a variety of environments. For example, in sport work, a bite to the left biceps is a targeted point value. Because of where our dogs might be operating, in a walled room, for instance, with the bad guy leaning against one of the walls and his left arm inside a doorway, the dog may not be able to get to that hidden arm. We do teach the dogs to target, but they have to learn to improvise.

And that's something that we work on throughout the entire time. We are always putting the dogs in weird positions. As the guys in the bite suit, we move at the last second. We may turn or crouch down or duck out of the way or raise a knee up and lean back or do anything that forces the dog to take what he can get, basically.

We'll also do things such as wrestling with the dog—putting a little bit of pinching or grabbing or twisting pressure on a dog's legs to teach him to keep his legs out of the way. Eventually we'll get to the point that, while he's engaged, he's got his legs tucked kind of back behind him, keeping them out of the way, something that the bad guy can't grab and try to break. Or if the guy does grab hold of him and starts to injure him, maybe the dog regrips on whatever hand, weapon, or object is attacking or hurting him, and goes after that.

If the scenario presents itself in which the dog can basi-

The author, two weeks before joining the Navy, atop the World Trade Center in NYC, aptly wearing a SEAL T-shirt.

The author and "Bud" the dog that started it all.

The author in headdress in central Iraq.

The author on patrol with the acrobat-ninja dog Luke.

The author in front of the U.S.S. *Cole* after it was attacked in Yemen.

SEAL Team 3 Echo platoon, post oil platform takedown two days prior to ground war commencing in Iraq.

The author with Barco, the
uphill-runaway-freight-train of a dog.

Wayne doing what he does best.

Lloyd with Cairo.

Lloyd and Cairo on watch.

Lloyd sending Cairo off to grab an insurgent.

Training in
bitework,
notice the deep
full grip of the
dogs mouth.

Aaron and Castor after detonating one of his life-saving finds.

Dave and Samson,
winning hearts and minds.

The social nature of
these dogs is of the
utmost importance.

Samson and the famous Elmo toy that became his favorite.

Dave and Samson getting some much needed rest.

MULTI PURPOSE CA

Aaron and Castor pose next to the company logo.

Treadmills aren't just for humans.

Wayne and his arch nemesis Luke, putting water under the bridge during a long training exercise.

The author during a sequence of events from the window training scenario that didn't quite go as planned.

An MPC and his handler getting ready to do some helo operations.

Gearing up for some cold weather detection exercises.

The "company" logo.

Luke smiling at
the photographer.

Dave and Samson getting ready to load up and
get after it.

Samson playing the role of
"hood ornament."

MPC and handler
getting ready to clear
an Afghan village.

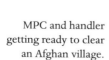

Cairo gets his workout in for the day.

Too cool for school . . .

Curt and Odin after a long night of work.

MPC and his handler fresh off an Afghan operation.

Retired MPC with his handler on a wintery R & R hike.

MPC and his handler on a CH-47 helo during insert.

MPC and his handler after a long night of combat operations in Afghanistan.

The retired dog Arko, wounded in combat and almost ten years old, but still very capable.

The author with Carlos, the dog that protected his handler even when his own life was in the balance.

Curt and Odin pre operation.

Curt and Odin getting
ready to clear a tunnel.

Odin charging ahead,
sniffing out the enemy.

Odin showing off his goggles,
a much needed piece of gear
to combat the dust and sand
for our K9s.

Odin on a
munitions cache hunt
after an ATV insert.

Odin ready to go
as usual.

Odin alerting on an
explosive find.

Curt and Odin about to load up for a raid.

An MPC and his handler atop a mountain.

Circling the wagons after a long patrol.

cally circle around back and get the guy in the triceps area, we'll teach a dog to do that as well, because it's incredibly difficult to fight a dog when he's got you by the back of the arm. You can't really grab him.

And so we ratchet up all these different types of targeting and pressure on the dog so that he is engaged in increasing apprehension training over the course of his entire life. And as his mental maturity can afford it, we put a little bit of extra pressure on him so that if he has to go into a building and fight, say, a six-foot-four, 240-pound linebacker on heroin, he's used to getting yelled at and punched and kicked and thrown against the wall. And that's all part of the game to him, basically, and it's not going to freak him out. He's not going to pop off, let go, and run away. He's been conditioned and trained to take that amount of pressure.

Similar to working through offensive and defensive drives, we have to be incredibly experienced, very patient, and very knowledgeable in reading the dog and knowing how much pressure to put on, when to raise the level and when to back off. Especially in the first year of that dog's life, it is very, very easy to ruin a good dog by pushing him and going too fast, putting too much pressure on him too early.

And sometimes it's difficult because you'll get dogs that are just firecrackers. They're really, really advanced. They're mentally more mature than they should be for their age. Maybe they're physically a little bigger than you would think or that you would expect, and you can get caught up in pushing them a little too far. But it's imperative that you don't, or you can have a detrimental effect on the dog and ruin him.

Again, the entire goal is a nonlethal neutralization of a

threat. I want to see the dog push through, come with forward aggression, and continue, to see the fight through the end—to control but not to kill.

I have to admit that as serious as this work is for me, I take a lot of pleasure in creating and participating in these on-site exercises. A lot of our terrain-adaptability training takes place in the numerous mountain ranges of our beautiful country. Because so many of the dogs are deployed with teams in Afghanistan, this is a pretty decent mock-up of what they'll encounter when there—both handler and dog. Just thinking about the feeling of driving along in an ATV at thirty-five to forty mph up a mountain pass with the goddamn dogs keeping up with us for eight hundred yards of elevation gain over the course of three-quarters of a mile gives you an appreciation for these dogs. They lope along in that classic herder stride, a combination of seemingly effortless athletic grace and fierce determination that gets my heart pumping in awe and pride.

I also have to say that I feel a bit of envy as well watching these dogs work at the peak of their powers. I spent years operating with SEAL Team 3 out of Coronado, California, completing multiple deployments to the Middle East, and loved every minute of it. It was an incredibly intense, fast-paced, and rewarding career that challenged me constantly but made me realize who I was. I left SEAL Team 3 and went to be an advanced training instructor at SQT (SEAL Qualification Training). I spent about eighteen months there, and during a training trip to a desert environment ended up contracting Valley Fever. Valley Fever is a fungal infection of the lungs that spreads like mold and scars your lung tissue permanently, to the point that you lose lung capacity. After recovering from that as much as my body was able to, I transferred over to BUD/S to be an instructor. I spent almost four years there selecting, teaching, and forging some of the finest warriors our nation has to offer. It was during that time that I learned as much as I could and have always admired what they brought to the table as a force-protection enhancement. While I can't be part of those forces working overseas, I still do my best, but I have to admit my somewhat-diminished physical capacity hasn't always been easy for me to live with.

Just because I'm no longer in the navy and not a member of SEAL Team, that doesn't mean that I've lost some of my competitive spirit or that I lack the kind of camaraderie I enjoyed as a SEAL Team member. My good friend Wayne—who is the guy I mentioned earlier in regard to the decoy work and being able to stand a dog down with his posture—was formerly a navy Search and Rescue (S & R) corpsman and is one hell of a guy, a man who has taught me a lot about dogs and is one of the real friends I've got in this life. I've got plenty of buddies, but just a few friends, and Wayne is one of them. We frequently work together in training MWDs, and Wayne brings a wealth of experience and insight into the mix.

Wayne grew up mostly in Florida and spent a lot of his early years in the swamps tracking and hunting wild hogs using dogs. I don't know of anyone else who can read a dog like Wayne can, and I also don't know anyone else who can work as a decoy any better than him. He's also a trainer, and one of the German shepherd dogs he had was titled in seven or eight different disciplines, which is an almost unheard-of accomplishment.

Wayne seems to have a preternatural sense of anticipation about what a dog is doing and thinking of doing. One night a few years ago, Wayne and I were on an apprehension training exercise with a group of about six dogs and handlers. We'd head up the mountains in advance of the dogs, be on comms with the handlers and another of our assistants. We'd be several miles out ahead of these men and dogs, and then we'd radio back when we'd selected a good hideout. The dogs would come into human odor and alert their handlers, get the *reviere* command, and dogs and handlers would come looking for us. We were suited up, of course, often in a middleweight suit with a neoprene underlayer—kind of like a wetsuit. That bottom layer offered additional padding but was also slick, making it harder for the dogs to grab hold when their teeth penetrated the outer part of the suit. After the first five dogs successfully got us, we were taking a break and shooting the shit.

It generally takes the dogs twenty to thirty minutes to cover the few miles between our find position and their release point. We did a debrief of the previous dog, taking notes so that we could do a full-blown evaluation of both dog and handler at the completion of the exercise. Wayne was next up as the decoy, and I looked at him and said, "You know who's coming, don't you?"

He nodded. "Yes, I do," he said, sounding both a bit prideful and on edge.

Luke was notorious for being the most acrobatic dog of that training group. If dogs could be gymnasts, Luke would have been the equivalent of both the Hamm brothers. The things this dog could do with his body, how he could flex, twist, and contort himself to make sure that his mouth was pointed in the right direction, were becoming legendary. The other thing about Luke was that he was damn smart. So, as a decoy, one of the challenges in catching Luke is that he was always really, really good at feinting and faking. He'd come at you, looking for sure like he was going to come at you hard, low, and left, and then right at the last split second, he'd switch it up and catch us off guard. As a decoy, you take pride in not being knocked down, because you do it so often that you kind of get good and you get comfortable, and then you start to get a little cocky, like, *This dog's not going to take me down.* Then Luke comes along, of course.

I said, "I bet you can't *esquive* Luke." *Esquive* is a French term that means to "dodge" or "sidestep" someone or something.

Wayne shook his head. "Bullshit. I'll *esquive* him all fucking day long."

So I said, "Okay, lets bet dinner on it. Winner's choice."

After a few minutes, I climbed to a little ridge where I could see better. It was a fairly well-lit night, quite a full moon, bright and close. Over the comms, I'd heard, "Dog out," about fifteen minutes before, so it was going to be just a few minutes until the action started. I sat there thinking, *All right, I can't wait to see this.*

Keep in mind: Wayne is not just one hell of a decoy. He's just the best decoy I've ever seen. He's so quick on his feet that I thought that if anybody had a chance to *esquive* Luke, it was Wayne. And I thought he honestly had a pretty good chance of *esquive*-ing Luke. When I saw Luke coming, I was a little disappointed. He was charging at him from much the same direction that an earlier dog, Duke, had come at me. I knew Wayne had seen how that had gone down—one of those times when I thought my arm was going to be crushed—and he'd have the advantage of seeing my mistake.

Suddenly, still running at close to full tilt, Luke didn't come uphill at Wayne; instead, he went around a few scrub bushes from the windward side and buttoned up back around. As a result, Wayne had to spin around real quick. As any good soldier knows, it's important to take the high ground, and that's exactly what Luke did. He took Wayne completely off guard, hit him right in the chest, and just pancaked my good friend's ass. Wayne is six feet two and weighs between 220 and 225 pounds, and Luke blitzed him like he was a bag full of leaves.

Wayne managed to get up and finish out the scenario, but afterward he was reluctant to own up to his loss.

"I knocked that one on purpose. I didn't want the dog to get hurt."

Whatever.

"Dude," I said to Wayne, "don't give me that BS excuse. I want my dinner."

Wayne made good on his promise, and I also had good ammunition to bust his balls with for the next two weeks. The combination of Luke's cunning and strength was extremely impressive.

Sometimes the dogs and their ability to use their bite strength have unintended consequences for those of us who train them.

Along with the mountain-terrain exercises, we also have to simulate urban ones. Given the nature of contemporary warfare, building searches are a common part of an MWD's duties. Fortunately, we have access to a number of compounds. One day, I set up a scenario that I thought would trip up the dogs with a combination of environmental factors. On this training day, we were on a compound that was spread out over two to three acres with approximately eight different buildings scattered across that space. It was in the foothills of some Southern California mountains, and the setting included heavy concentrations of vegetation, good-sized trees, and plenty of scrub. The environment was a close approximation of what they'd encounter in Afghanistan.

As usual, we took the dogs and handlers, six of each in this case, and we decided that our hiding spot was going to be in the largest of the buildings on site—an open-bay barracks, similar to what you might see at boot camp. There were three such buildings on the training ground, and each had a hundred or so two-tiered beds, a couple of common-area rooms, a large mess/kitchen area, some storage rooms, and, most critical to this exercise, two larger shower areas and bathrooms. In other words, these were sprawling buildings with multiple good hiding spots.

I explained the training exercise to the handlers by saying, "Okay, you guys are going to patrol in, cordon off security, and go into this building and try to find a high-value target in there."

That target was me in a bite suit.

This was a daytime exercise, but I had blacked out all the windows, so it was dark in there. A dog's vision isn't quite as negatively affected as ours is by going from a bright room to a pitch-black room, but it absolutely is similar. I selected a hiding spot in that shower area, as far from the building's entry point as possible. To add to the confusion caused by the dark, I also turned on all the showerheads with the water running full blast. In my mind this was going to be a major obstacle, the equivalent of the dogs working through a waterfall outdoors. Only in this case, it was pitch-black in there.

I squatted against a wall, breathing the moist air, confident that I'd have plenty of time to wait and likely have a dog or two fail to find me at all.

I was wrong.

Within a few minutes, the first dog came blasting out of the darkness to pile-drive me. My intention to make it tougher on the dog by having the water running turned into a serious disadvantage for me. I was in a bite suit, wrestling with a wet dog, trying to keep my footing on a slippery tile floor, waiting for the dog's handler to find me to get the damn dog off me. Even though I trained these dogs myself at times, by this point in their training, some nineteen months in, they only obeyed their handlers—as they should.

I don't know if words can adequately describe the feelings of anticipation and dread that you experience when you're in a situation like that, knowing that at any second, a sixty-to-eighty-pound monster is going to steamroller you. It is time for more than sweaty palms, let me tell you, but the thrill of it never gets old. That's especially true when the dogs and handlers do such a stellar job, like they did on this particular day. Wayne and I had switched on and off being the decoy, and we both agreed that we'd been foiled and the dogs had won the battle that day. My pride wasn't wounded, but it was tough to walk off the field of battle with such sore and rapidly swelling forearms, hands, and legs.

As I mentioned earlier, the dogs can be seriously injured or killed if they are turned loose to apprehend someone who is near a window or on a roof or some other elevated structure.

The dogs are kept on leash during some of the exercises and, depending on the situation, when in the field and actually working. The handlers have to make decisions about when to release them—and it generally varies when a dog indicates or shows a sign that they've gotten the scent trail of a human. During these training exercises for apprehension, I'm doing a lot of different things, including evaluating the handlers' decisions. I want them to be able to make swift and appropriate choices, obviously, and the only way to do that is to make them work through multiple scenarios time and time again.

We'd traveled to another compound-type training area, this one in the American Southeast, among stands of loblolly pines. The buildings in this compound were constructed of cinder block, and small windows were formed from blocks that had been knocked out of the walls. The discarded blocks lay on the ground inside the structures. For this exercise, I told the handlers to keep the dogs on leash until the moment they thought best. What I was hoping would happen, a kind of teachable moment, was that a handler would release a dog prematurely. I'd been standing on a few of those blocks, with my body half inside the room and half hanging out the window. My plan was that as soon as a dog inserted itself into the room, I'd jump out the window and then turn around to catch the dog that had followed me out the window and onto the grassy area below.

The point, of course, would be to make it clear to that handler that he'd made a poor choice. Not only had the bad guy evaded capture, the MWD had been hurt in that fall from the window. In the exercise, of course, the window was only thirty or so inches off the ground, so no harm would come to the dog.

Even after all these years of working with these dogs, I can still underestimate just how fast they can get to you. On the first go-round, I barely scrambled out of the window fully intact before the dog was literally nipping at my heels. It came tearing after me from around the back, as he had caught wind of me and had scurried out the door on the side. I was just glad that I was able to illustrate for the handler what might have happened without putting a dog's health at risk. I chose my profession and the risks that go along with it. Dogs don't get the same choice, and as I've said repeatedly, the dogs are doing what they are bred to do and take a great deal of pleasure in doing it. They don't get to exercise the same level of choice that we humans do, but, still, I take the responsibility to provide dogs that are sound in their training and in their health.

Just like humans, dogs occasionally develop nagging overuse injuries during the course of their training, and they sometimes either get left behind entirely from their "classmates" or more often they just lag behind for a day or two to recuperate; sometimes they rest for an entire training cycle and join another class already in the pipeline.

I hadn't really made the connection between the apprehension work we do and the feelings I experience when in the bite suit. I'm eager to make sure that the dogs are safe and in the best possible shape to help keep our soldiers, sailors, and marines safe. Even knowing what it feels like when those teeth penetrate the bite suit, I don't have any sympathy for the bad guys who encounter these dogs in the flesh.

I love the work I do, and I know how important it is to take the time to get things done right. We work hard and have some fun as well, but I absolutely refuse to cut corners.

At one point, I received word about how the dogs were doing. This story confirmed what I believed: we were on the right track and the dogs we provided were making a difference.

The moon sat just above the ridge of the mountain as we descended into a cutback that would lead us down into a valley. The boys adjusted their gear; the hike down into the valley was crisscrossed with barren loose rock and dense thorny brush along nothing more than what equated to a goat path. There had been a lot of activity in the area lately, the ground giving away constant sign of foot traffic, which had kicked loose the rock underfoot. The terrain glowed with a greenish tint as we looked through our NVGs, studying the lay of the land before us, everyone alert for the slightest hint of danger. Reno was out front, his muscled lean body moving with little effort, his eyes alert, ears perked at every sound; his breath, as he exhaled, created a small vortex of hot humid air as it interacted with the cold dry air that surrounded him. I had been Reno's partner now for a little over a year, and the bond between my dog and me was something that ran deep and was hard to truly explain; quite simply put, I loved him and trusted my very life to him.

We were moving toward a target that was positioned on the other side of a small river that ran along the bottom of the valley floor. The area, according to our intel, was alive with enemy activity; recent reports had a bomb maker in the area, whom we had been hunting for months. He had been involved in several IED incidents that had claimed American lives; if we had anything to do with it after tonight, he would no longer be able to hurt another one of our brothers or sisters. The guys had packed light; the elevation change was thousands of feet, spread out over a dozen miles, and we had to get in and out in this cycle of darkness. Covering a dozen miles under normal circumstances is relatively easy; doing it in the dark with a massive elevation change and carrying fifty pounds of gear, along with the always-present chance of contact can be downright exhausting. Reno moved with purpose, his incredible senses scanning the area around him, looking for the possibility of his second favorite thing in the world—a ball. Reno had no idea that he was out front leading the way to warn us of the danger of an IED; he simply knew that if he found explosive odor, a ball would magically appear out of thin air and he would get to carry it around like a trophy for a while.

My knowledge base of explosive and human-odor movement had grown a hundredfold over the last year. I knew that to best use Reno's natural capabilities, I had to put him into the best position possible to take advantage of the situation, keeping mission requirements and limitations in mind. I looked at the terrain and calculated wind direction, wind speed, temperature, humidity, elevation changes, terrain formations, barometric pressure, and vegetation types and densities. Most of my concentration was on the dog; subtle changes in his body language could give me large clues as to what was going on around us. It was up to John, walking just behind me, to scan the terrain and guide us in the right direction. We rounded a corner, and the wind was suddenly blowing directly in our faces as we moved down the ridge, a stiff cold breeze that chilled me to the bone. Reno's head lifted slightly as he sniffed the new flow of air; I pictured thousands of molecules being processed by his olfactory system, and a sense of calm overcame me. He was not worried, so neither was I.

The next few hours wore on. The downhill portion of this track was starting to rub the front of my toes raw; a lot of weight at a steep angle over time will do that to even the most seasoned feet. The trail doubled back on itself as we nearly reached the valley floor. The wind at our backs as we moved forward sent a chill running down my spine, yet not from the cold. Everything I had learned over the last year screamed at me: this situation was developing into an almost worst-case scenario for Reno. The wind was cold and running fast from behind us down a narrow ravine that would open into the valley, pushing any odor away from us until we were on top of it. Not good.

I signaled the guys to move back a bit as Reno and I pushed forward. I would be lying if I said that my heartbeat was not elevated. I was about to move through a choke point in the terrain in hostile enemy territory that was densely covered with a thick thorn-bearing bush that neither made the path quiet or easy to see through. I gave the command for Reno to move forward and search for any hint of human or explosive odor. My weapon was raised and pointed in the general direction I expected a threat, as I watched my boy search the area. His nose was down, sucking in all available odor, his tail up and wagging as he crisscrossed the path and deeper into the choke point.

I moved forward slowly, step-by-step, as I watched him work. Eventually we were through the high-threat area. Reno had never signaled a threat. I took a deep breath and smiled at John. He simply signaled to me in sign language, Fuck you.

I returned the gesture and we pushed forward again; I started to relax as we moved along the valley floor, my eyes trained on Reno, knowing that John was acting as my eyes and that the rest of the boys were on their game, also. We were getting close to the target when all of a sudden I stopped dead in my tracks. Reno's head had snapped around, his tail starting to waggle a hundred miles an hour as he worked his way back toward me. He was working the wind, obviously in explosive odor. With the wind at our backs, I had no idea how far back the explosive was. My breathing stopped as I scanned the ground around me with one eye and watched Reno with the other, adrenaline rushing through my system like white-hot lava. Reno sat two feet to my right and five feet in front of me, eyes focused on the ground, tail wagging furiously.

I quickly calculated what had happened; the wind had pushed the odor in a narrow scent cone out in front of us; by the time explosive molecules were available for Reno to pick up, he had already walked past the buried IED. My mind ran through a thousand possibilities before I settled on the most likely scenario being a pressure plate in our path with the explosives buried just off the track but still plenty close enough to kill anyone standing on that plate. I carefully circled around the area and then called Reno to me, making sure he would not cross the area where I was guessing the explosives lay. I tossed him a ball and gave him a quick pat as my heart and breathing rate returned to near normal. We took a quick GPS reading, marked the location, and moved on. I turned to John as I normally did, expecting our normal sign language, and received a thumbs-up instead. To be truthful, that gesture scared me.

It took us another hour to reach our target location, which proved to be yet another wrong lead or, at the very least, untimely information. The villagers were on edge. The call would go out to all local fighters, so it was time to leave, and fast. Our extraction point was at the leeward edge of the next ridge, but we were running short on time and moved with purpose. Ten minutes into our climb out we were related information that a large group of Taliban fighters were descending on the valley. An hour later the back of my legs were burning, my heart racing, the cold nothing more than an afterthought as my body superheated. Reno was starting to slow down, even though he is a specimen of a dog, in incredible shape, his muscles shredded from countless hours of training in environments that simulate our theater of operation.

I had to call a halt, resting a few minutes while Reno caught his breath. We set up a perimeter quickly. Each man was on edge, yet to look at them, they all looked calm and relaxed, a smile on a couple of faces as sweat clung to their clothes. It is at times like this that I reflect upon the company I was keeping on this mountainside in some third-world country, being hunted by a number of enemies that far outnumbered us: I would be nowhere else in the world; each one was my brother.

Reno drank some water from my canteen, his tongue dripping water all over me as he licked my face quickly. I smiled and pushed him away gently, then patted his side quietly. I gave him a few minutes, then put him back to work. We moved back up the mountain, pushing ourselves to reach safety. A few minutes thereafter I thanked my stars above that I had given him that break. I had my eyes off of Reno as I tried to catch myself as my foot slipped on the loose, rocky terrain. As I looked up he was locked, his body ridged, as his ears pushed forward, a slight quiver in his rear left leg.

He was in human odor, the greatest reward my dog had.

I instantly lifted my M-4 as my eyes scanned the terrain

above us; I knew without looking that John and the others guys were moving as soon as my weapon came up. Reno took off at a dead sprint and disappeared twenty feet to our left; seconds afterward screams came from the area. I moved forward, scanning the environment as I moved, wanting to come to Reno's aid as soon as possible but unwilling to leave behind my tactical sense. I heard three shots ring out, as a Taliban fighter tried to exit the shallow cut that they had been hiding in. His companion was locked in a fight with Reno; the dog was destroying his opponent, blood quickly covering the man's clothes. I called Reno out of the fight and squeezed off several rounds as the man reached for his weapon. We quickly searched the area before moving on, our pace even quicker than before; the gunfire for sure had given away our position. Legs and lungs burned, the elevation taking its toll, as we finally reached our destination.

Sitting on the edge of that mountain waiting for our ride, I looked back at the last few hours. I patted Reno's head. Twice tonight he had saved my life; twice I owed him yet another debt of gratitude. His body shivered slightly as the cold wind bit into him; now that we weren't moving, the cold settled quickly. I pulled off my coat and wrapped him in it, pulling his body against mine to keep him warm. . . . Tonight he had saved my life; tonight he had saved my brothers' lives.

Every graduating class has its stars, the students whose performance in the classroom or on the playing fields makes it clear that they are going to succeed at whatever they choose to do. Sometimes they live up to those expectations, and sometimes they don't. The same is true with the dogs that we train. Every time a governmental agency, a military group, or even a private individual looking for a protection dog comes to view the prospects that I have, I mentally compile a list of the dogs that I think are the sure things among the bunch, the ones that are undoubtedly in my mind the ones worthy of the purchase price.

As often as not, my mental rankings are a lot like those preseason polls and predictions in football: some of my prognostications prove true and nearly as many prove to be off target. Everybody who views dogs during these workouts and showings sees something slightly different. I'm biased, of course. I think that what I see in the dogs is the "truth" about them, but as the saying goes, the customer is always right. I guess because I've been involved in the breeding, training, and sale of dogs for more than fifteen years now, you'd think it would be easy for me to say good-bye to the dogs I've worked with. In one sense that's true. I'm glad to see them go and do what they were bred, born, and trained to accomplish, but I'm always going to have some emotional attachment to the dogs. As much as I've talked about them and their abilities, these dogs aren't machines. They have distinctive personalities.

One dog in particular, who shall remain nameless, got my attention very early on in the process. Immediately after we brought him over to the United States, I went to his crate to let him out. It was like I'd released a Tasmanian devil. That dog got up on his hind legs, spun in tornadic circles, snapped his jaws like the maniac he was, and generally said to me, *Hello, my name is Havoc.* Essentially, he was announcing to me that he was going to be a handful just to get the most basic obedience into him. As much as I've talked about what near-perfect physical specimens these dogs are, the fact that they've been bred to preserve that high energy and tenacious-ness necessary to go at it in hostile environments means these dogs are seldom docile. I developed a tremendous amount of respect for the spastic Tas-like dog I mentioned above, but I can't say that I ever really developed a bond of affection for him.

That wasn't the case with one of the first dogs to work with a SEAL Team. Rocket was like one of those kids you may have admired (or hated) in your high school class. He was good-looking, athletic, and genial. All the other kids liked him, the teachers and administrators got along well with him, but he never seemed to put on airs. Rocket is like that. You'll read more about his contributions in the field, but it's important that you get a picture of the human/canine relationship and how it functions, as well.

For example, on Rocket's second deployment to northern Afghanistan, near the Northwest Frontier Province of Pakistan, he and his handler, Brent, arrived at a firebase that was still under construction. This was in January of 2007, in the dead of winter, and the troops were living in open base tents while the buildings were being completed. To put it mildly, life there was a mixture of dealing with the ball-shattering cold and frozen tedium. Handlers have to be very careful about how they integrate themselves into the SEAL Teams and with other military. They have to be sensitive to the fact that each of their comrades brings a different set of associations and experiences to being in close contact with an MWD. Some of the men are fearful, others curious, others disdainful out of ignorance about the roles the dogs will eventually play, and so on. For handler and dog, it's just like being a newbie in any situation; you have to earn whatever respect you're going to be afforded by your teammates.

Brent wanted to make sure that everybody understood from the get-go that Rocket was there to be a help and not to be an impediment. He also let them know that his relationship with Rocket was a kind of one-off—that the two of them had forged a real bond in the nearly two years they'd worked together before being deployed. In order to respect the other troops and their safety and their personal space and gear, Brent and Rocket would require segregated housing—their own room, basically. After having this discussion, the Seabees who were there were assigned to build a partition and a door within the tent where Brent and Rocket were to rack out.

As luck would have it, the pair was already assigned to a tent where the Seabees were quartered. In the first couple of days, before the wall could be built, Rocket did what dogs do: he foraged for food. The Seabees had a few snacks that Rocket sniffed out and consumed. Brent apologized, and he could tell that a few of the guys were cool with it, but others looked a little anxious. Two things were clear: they weren't going to complain too loudly, and they certainly weren't going to confront the fierce-looking dog. A compromise was reached. Until the wall and door could go up to keep Rocket away from their stuff, they'd put it out of reach.

Brent noticed that as the days went on, when some of the Seabees and other guys in the tent had to get out of bed in the middle of the night to do a watch, they'd come back and find Rocket sacked out in their rack snoring. At first Brent thought that they didn't dare wake up and roust Rocket out of their rack because they were afraid of him, but after finding a couple of guys sleeping on the floor while Rocket happily snoozed more comfortably, he asked them about it. They said that they didn't mind Rocket sleeping in their beds; they kind of liked the idea of having him around. Rocket became a kind of mascot, a four-legged roommate, and he took full advantage of the attention and affection he got. Not every MWD had his temperament, but there was just something about his big-eared and quizzical expression that let you know that he was easygoing when off duty. The only complaint the guys had was that Rocket sometimes busted ass in the middle of everybody, a product of them sneaking him foods that he wasn't accustomed to getting. Not much different from the rest of the guys, in reality.

The wall that was supposed to keep Rocket from the remainder of the guys never really got built. At first the framing went up, then it was sheeted, but no door was hung. The Seabees and others confessed that they liked having Rocket around, and they knew that once that door went up, he'd be separated from them. In time, the wall came down, later they guys were told by the officer in charge (OIC) that it had to go back up and a door had to be installed. Once again, the guys came up with excuses to delay the building of it. Finally the wall went up, but for the duration of that deployment, no door was ever hung and Rocket was free to mingle with the rest of them. Maybe he was like having a bit of home for some of the guys, but I do know that just as much as that, it was a tribute to Rocket's amiability. His big brown eyes melted a lot of hearts and earned him his share of treats. By the end of deployment, Brent told me, he had a list of names a mile long of guys who wanted first dibs on one of Rocket's puppies.

Some say that dogs are nature's greatest con artists, that they've finagled for themselves a pretty soft gig compared to most animals. They're certainly not parasites, and the kind of symbiosis we and canines have negotiated over the years has truly proved beneficial, just as Rocket's role both in the field and on station did. So much has been written about the complexity and the history of the human/canine relationship that I won't spend any real time debating the con-artist issue. All I will say is that whatever ease dogs have accrued as a result of their domestication, we've frequently asked a lot from them in return. That's particularly true as it applies to our long history of using them in warfare. Another way to look at it is this: the people we allow to take advantage of our kindness are generally not strangers; they're usually family members and close friends. We benefit from those relationships, or have benefited from them, in the past and hope to in the future. So really, nobody is truly being conned. You can also look at it from the dogs' perspective. We've taken advantage of their good nature, their desire to share their companionship with us, and we've used them to our advantage. Everything's a trade-off, I suppose, but in my estimation, we humans have come out far ahead in the canine/human transaction.

Because dogs have a shared sense of community, they likely first adapted themselves to living near and then later with humans. They became part of a shared existence with us, and the transition from a nomadic existence to one more rooted in place led them to eventually have to share another seemingly inevitable part of human life—warfare. Because of what battle involves—detection and apprehension, among other activities—we couldn't have selected a better animal teammate. As I've mentioned, dogs and their keen sense of smell, sight (primarily motion detection, which is aided by the long-snouted breeds like Malinois having roughly a 250-to-270-degree field of vision due to their wide-spaced eyes), and hearing make them ideal guard dogs.[1]

Whatever warlike purpose dogs have served, from sentry duty to detection, they have a long history of being employed in some capacity. As far back as ancient Egypt (if we are to believe that some of their artwork is accurate), dogs were used as both offensive and defensive forces. Some Egyptian murals depict dogs being unleashed on Egyptian warriors' enemies. Similarly, the Greeks recorded a dog's contributions on a mural celebrating the Battle of Marathon against the Persians. Written accounts by the Roman writers and historians Plutarch and Pliny exist, and Strabo, a Greek historian, described the dogs being "protected with coats of mail."[2] From their use by nearly every ancient city-state through Attila the Hun, William the Conqueror, and succeeding generations of English rulers and leaders; the Spanish conquistadors; Napoleon; and Frederick the Great, dogs have served loyally. A frequently cited example of war dogs and their loyalty is Napoleon's writing in his memoirs, "I walked over the battlefield and among the slain, a poodle killed bestowing a last lick upon his dead friend's face. Never had anything on any battlefield caused me a like emotion."[3] Today, many of us think of the French poodle as the epitome of the spoiled, prissy canine, but poodles have a long history as military working dogs.

Here in North America, Native Americans also used canines as watchdogs. Like several other groups, they also used a dog's strength and endurance to their advantage. Dogs hauled packs and served as draft animals, just as horses did. European settlers and their successors used dogs against the Indians. Benjamin Franklin was involved in organizing the Pennsylvania militia against the Native Americans and wrote a letter proposing how they might be used, based on his knowledge of how the Spanish utilized them in Mexico.[4]

John Penn, the grandson of William Penn, also suggested using dogs against the "savages," calling for the militiamen to be paid an allowance for the use of their dogs and stating that the owners should be responsible for leashing and leading their canines in pursuit of the enemy. In both Franklin's and Penn's cases, there's no evidence that their suggestions were implemented. The same was true of a proposal brought forward during the Revolutionary War. Some evidence exists that dogs were used as messengers during the Civil War, but this was mostly the result of an individual soldier bringing his own dog to battle on his own initiative and not any kind of sanctioned use. Dogs did serve as mascots, and many of their names are included in honor roles. Several statues commemorating the Battle of Gettysburg depict dogs, but they most likely only served as mascots.[5]

One of the more fascinating stories to emerge out of canine military history comes from World War I. The United States didn't enter into the war until 1917, of course, after years of fierce and often fruitless battles. Trench warfare was a serious and deadly business, but it often seemed pointless, with victories measured in yards of territory gained. The trenches themselves could be another kind of horror, and dogs helped alleviate at least one element of that. Jack Russell terriers roamed the trenches attacking the rats that plagued the soldiers and their food supplies. More important, though, was the work that so-called Mercy Dogs did as a part of the Red Cross's efforts to help the wounded. Red Cross institutions in multiple countries utilized dogs to carry medical supplies, find the wounded, and offer comfort to those who wouldn't survive their injuries.

Because many of the MWDs we use today can have their lineages traced back to Germany and the war dogs of that nation, I was particularly struck by stories of how the *Sanitatshunde*— "sanitary dogs," as the Germans referred to these canine Red Cross workers—were trained to find the wounded among the battlefield casualties that lay littered across a no-man's-land. These dogs were trained to go out into that legendary zone, with water or alcohol in canteens and with packs strapped to their bodies, to offer the injured what was often some small comfort before the men died. More important, the dogs were sent out to identify the location of the wounded, most often at night, and return with some token—a cap, a helmet, or other identifier—and then lead a handler to the site of the wounded man so that he could be recovered. This kind of human detection and the training methodologies and signals humans and canines shared to communicate a find are all very much like what we do today with our MWDs.

It's estimated that the Germans used a total of nearly thirty thousand dogs during World War I. They had six thousand on the front lines and four thousand in reserve at the beginning of the war. Most other European nations involved in the conflict also utilized dogs to varying degrees. We'll never know the actual number of dogs involved, nor the number of casualties among these canine helpers. It's a little easier to know the extent to which dogs helped support U.S. troop activities during the Great War.

Because we didn't have a long history of using dogs in battle, and possibly because we entered the war later and didn't see all the other ways that other countries utilized dogs in World War I (as ambulance dogs pulling two-wheeled carts, for example), our use of canines as we entered into the

War to End All Wars was essentially nonexistent. We eventually used dogs trained by the French and British, but a program to train American dogs and to supply our troops with them was never implemented. We did, however, supply the French army with four hundred dogs, which served in the alpine regions as draft animals, helping to haul artillery shells with far greater efficiency than humans, mules, and horses could.

One of the primary uses in which the other combatants employed canines was as messenger dogs. Obviously, communication between troops on the front lines and their leaders at the rear are crucial in any military campaign. Often, more established lines of communication, in this case, literal lines for telephones, broke down. Human soldiers often served as messengers, but they not only were larger targets, fatigued more easily, and were slower than dogs, they were also considered a more valuable military asset to be utilized offensively. As a result, dogs served in that vital role, carrying written messages and carrier pigeons in a specially designed saddlebag from position to position. One French messenger dog, a mixed breed named Satan, earned great distinction for his bravery and was eventually immortalized in a short story used in schools in the United States in the 1920s. In a textbook entitled *Junior High School Literature: Book Two*, the editors, William H. Elson and Christine M. Keck, included a short story by the writer Ernest Harold Baynes.[6]

Baynes must have based his work on the story that was told of Satan coming to the rescue of a group of French soldiers near the town of Verdun. They were encamped at a small village near that famous city, and the Germans had circled them, cutting off their supply lines, their communications, and virtually any hope of surviving. In addition to not having working phones, the soldiers were without carrier pigeons, so no one in the French command knew their exact location or their plight. The Germans did, and they pounded their location with heavy artillery, taking an enormous toll on another so-called Lost Battalion. According to the account in Michael Lemish's book *War Dogs,* German soldiers later reported seeing a vision, a large-headed creature with wings.

What they actually saw was Satan, approaching the French position, with a carrier pigeon with its wings flapping on each of his sides. He also wore a gas mask as he maneuvered stealthily to avoid enemy fire. Satan was struck twice by German gunfire, but he managed to complete his mission and deliver the two carrier pigeons. Eventually, one of those birds successfully evaded being shot down, and later the French artillery responded to the German fusillade. Without that dog's courage and intelligence, as well as the intelligence contained in the message the bird carried, the battle would have been lost. As it was, the Germans were trumped.

In Baynes's version, Satan was a mixed breed, but the author identified him as the product of an English greyhound sire and a Scotch collie dam. That could seem to be a bit of English propaganda, but one thing is certain: the work of an English officer, E. H. Richardson, was so instrumental that he became known as the father of modern war-dog training. Later on, during both World War II and in Vietnam, the United States relied on British expertise and experience to assist us in developing programs that utilized military working dogs.

Satan wasn't the only dog to earn fame as a result of

experiences during World War I. Rin Tin Tin, the subject of a recent book by the renowned writer Susan Orleans, also has roots in the European battlefield. According to the legend, a German mascot pup, Rin Tin Tin, was discovered abandoned in a German trench by a group of American soldiers. His owner and trainer, Lee Duncan, claimed that this was the case. Some skeptics state that the dog that would later star in a series of American films—and was likely one of the main causes of the popularity of the German shepherd dog breed in the United States—was actually an offspring of an adult dog found in Germany. Regardless, Rin Tin Tin's box-office success (he was the top-grossing movie star of 1926) is as indisputable as is his impact on breeders and buyers.

Less well known is the pit bull Stubby, who an American soldier smuggled aboardship on his way to Europe to fight in late 1917. Stubby spent nineteen months overseas, and returned to a hero's welcome, eventually earning honors from the American Red Cross, the YMCA, and the American Legion, and was presented with a gold medal by General John Joseph "Black Jack" Pershing, the commander of the American Expeditionary Forces, on behalf of the American Humane Society. Three American presidents also met Stubby during the dog's lifetime.

The American public clearly liked the idea of dogs serving with our troops, but the military was less enthusiastic about the idea. Despite seeing what effect dogs had on the conduct of the war and the morale of soldiers and civilians alike, following World War I no branch of the American military created a formal program for training and using dogs on the field of battle between the end of the First World War and the beginning of World War II. The U.S. military had hired private contractors as early as the 1900s to drive sled dogs in the Alaska Territory. The famous Tenth Mountain Division, originally formed at Fort Lewis in Washington State and later relocated to Camp Hale in Colorado, also included dogsled drivers. Once the war was under way and more military activity, particularly the flying of planes, was taking place in Alaska, the USAF Tenth Air Rescue Squadron was supplied with as many as two hundred dogs to take on that mission of finding downed crews—both U.S. and Russian—on the route from Alaska to Siberia, as well as in Greenland.[7] The latter was part of the "Bolero Movement," ferrying planes to the North Atlantic as a prelude to the Allied invasion of Western Europe and the USAAF bombing campaign against the Nazis.

Obviously, Pearl Harbor changed a great deal for Americans. It did the same to a lesser degree for the country's dogs as well. That surprise attack, rumors of German spies coming ashore, and the acknowledged need for tremendous vigilance all combined to see dogs take on an expanded role within the United States as sentries. With so many vital installations, including the industries that made up the so-called war machine, and the ever-present threat of what we'd today call terrorist activity, the Coast Guard took the lead in deploying handler-dog teams along our vast shoreline. With everyone willing and wanting to contribute to the war effort, dog owners and dog lovers led a campaign to promote the use of dogs in wartime activities.

Several influential members of the canine community, including the director of the American Kennel Club, got together and established the Dogs for Defense (DFD) organization in

1942. It brought together professional and amateur trainers and breeders as well as private individuals who wanted to support the cause of utilizing dogs to a greater extent than ever before as a part of the American military. At first their efforts were met with resistance. The American military was reluctant to let civilians take the lead in establishing any kind of policy. Eventually, those barriers were overcome when the need for protection of military depots around the country became more of a priority. In July of 1942, Secretary of War Harold Stimson issued a directive calling for the quartermaster general to train dogs to serve a variety of functions beyond sentry duty. This would include search and rescue, hauling, detection/scouting patrols, and messengering. All the branches of the armed forces received the orders, but it was up to them to decide individually how many dogs to recruit and how to utilize them.

The U.S. Army Quartermaster Corps (QMC) took over from the Plant Protection Branch by September of 1942. The program, unofficially, was known as the K9 Corps early on, and the army adopted a part of that name with its K9 Section. Eventually the quartermaster general announced that the United States would need 125,000 dogs for the army, navy, marines, and Coast Guard combined. American citizens had already joined breeders and trainers in "volunteering" their dogs as part of the DFD programs. DFD had been providing dogs for the army, while the navy and marines briefly relied on private individuals and sources. All four branches, including the navy, eventually turned to the DFD as a source for suitable recruits.

The DFD established regional centers to accept the donations, and the dogs were considered gifts, with no promise made that the dogs would be returned—except if the dogs didn't meet the basic requirements. In the first two years, the DFD received forty thousand dogs; eventually about eighteen thousand passed initial inspection, and ten thousand actually saw duty. While those numbers may not seem particularly impressive, they *are* when you consider that this was an entirely volunteer program staffed by people whose only desire was to aid the war effort.

By August of 1942, dogs were patrolling the beach with their Coast Guard handlers. By the end of the first year of the combined efforts of the quartermaster general's office and the DFD, eighteen hundred teams were doing that work, with another eight hundred handlers being fully trained by the end of the war. Though initially the quartermaster general's office issued an Army Technical Manual bulletin identifying thirty-two potential breeds and crosses as candidates, by the end of 1944 they'd narrowed that field of candidates to seven breeds: "German shepherd, Doberman pinscher, Belgian sheepdog, collie, Siberian husky, malamute, and Eskimo dog."[8]

The main function of these Coast Guard units was eventually fully clarified. The Coast Guard was responsible for spotting trouble and reporting it. The army was in charge of protecting the coastline and turning back any hostile troops. By May of 1944, it became clear that no hostile invasion was forthcoming and that any acts of sabotage were unlikely. The coastline-protection program was drawn down, with the dogs then being transferred to the army.

Interestingly, one of the places that the army used as a

training ground for canines was named, ironically enough, Cat Island. Just off Gulfport, Mississippi, the environment was ideal for training dogs that might eventually serve in the Pacific theater. The island was also the site of a failed experiment to train a group of dogs to be offensive weapons—attack dogs. The program was once classified, but in recent years the PBS television show *The History Detectives,* the Biloxi-Gulfport *Sun Herald,* and various online outlets have featured stories on this unusual program.

A Swiss émigré by the name of William A. Pestre, a former Swiss army officer, sent a proposal to the War Department in 1942, claiming that he could train a group of dogs to attack Japanese positions. He believed that the dogs could either kill the enemy soldiers or cause enough of a distraction that the American soldiers would easily be able to take those positions. He suggested that the U.S. Army could recruit as many as twenty thousand to thirty thousand dogs for the effort. The army had already selected Cat Island as a training center, and it was run by the Army Ground Forces and not the Quartermaster Corps. Army Lieutenant Colonel A. R. Nichols was swayed by Pestre's arguments and agreed to get the program off the ground. Nichols insisted that the training be done in thirty days.

Pestre proved to be a very demanding and selective taskmaster. Of the four hundred dogs sent to him, he only approved of twelve for further training. That number was trimmed to nine—the only ones who would be acceptable as attack dogs. In order to train these dogs, he would need humans to act as "live bait," in this case, Japanese men, since the dogs needed to be trained to identify their distinctive odor.

This is where the story turns even more bizarre. Not only would it be, in my opinion, nearly impossible in three months to train dogs to do anything with the kind of precision necessary to accomplish any mission under battlefield circumstances, the program now necessitated the use of nontrained volunteers to act as what we would today call decoys.

Fortunately, or perhaps unfortunately, depending upon your attitude toward this program, Japanese-American soldiers were available for this duty; members of the 100th Infantry Battalion and the 442nd Combat Team were also in training on a nearby island at Camp Shelby. From among these *nisei* (Japanese-Americans) twenty-five volunteers were sent to Cat Island.⁹ The volunteers engaged in questionable training practices designed to get the dogs to attack them as stand-ins for the Japanese soldiers on whom the dogs would eventually be set loose. Pestre trained the dogs for three months and then put on a demonstration of the dogs' capabilities. It was a miserable failure. Either the dogs failed to attack the padded *nisei* with any kind of ferocity or they had to be led directly to them rather than track them. Pestre was given one other chance to prove the value of his program, but that wasn't good enough either to convince the army leadership that it had any military value. The program was terminated, despite Pestre's protests.

The idea of using dogs in a jungle environment wasn't abandoned. The marines suffered a high casualty rate in places like Guadalcanal and the other chain of islands that led to the Japanese mainland. The dense vegetation made them particularly prone to ambush and sniper fire. In November of 1942, the marines began a training program, aided by the

efforts of the Doberman Pinscher Club of America, to prepare dogs and handlers to serve on point during jungle
patrols. Again, the Dogs for Defense group served as the liai-
son between the dog clubs, private citizens, and the military. In
time, the marine dogs became known as Devil Dogs, a name
with origins dating back to World War I and the Germans'
description of the human marines they encountered in battle.

The Marine Corps treated the dogs like human soldiers in
one respect: they assigned them ranks. In this case, it was
based on length of service, from private first class to master
gunner sergeant after five years of duty. Dogs could also receive honorable or dishonorable discharges, all in the hope of
developing a fighting spirit among the canine corps. At first
these dogs were trained for typical canine sentry duty, but the
marines wanted the dogs to be combat participants, given the
nature of the work they did. In early 1943, a scout and messenger dog-training program began.

These early programs in the United States were instrumental in shaping later thinking. Both the leadership within
the army and marines realized very quickly that civilian
trainers who'd worked with dogs in police or private training
environments didn't have the tactical background to make
them effective in combat situations. As a result, drawing handlers from the troops became the preferred option. Another
lesson learned was that the fourteen weeks the marines spent
in training scout and messenger dogs could be too intensive.
Without proper rest and relaxation during training, the dogs'
performance actually degraded rather than improved. The
first Devil Dogs served in squads of four canines—three
scouts and one messenger dog—along with six men. Platoons

were comprised of three squads along with an officer, sixty-five men, and eighteen scout and messenger dogs.[10] The first deployments were in the Solomon Islands.

The army's Quartermaster Corps prepared 595 dogs for scouting duty to serve in the K9 Corps. Each of their squads consisted of eight dogs (four scouts and four messengers) with eight handlers. Seven units were attached to a corps or division in Europe, and eight in the Pacific. The Forty-second War Dog Platoon played a critical role in the Battle of the Bulge, and then its dogs worked as sentries at supply depots in Belgium. Others served guarding communications lines as well as leading infantry patrols. Similar to what I experienced, many men, after having dogs serve as scouts on patrol, reported that they never wanted to go out without canines and handlers again.

From the jungle heat and humidity of the Solomon Islands to the frozen tundra of Alaska to the fields and forests of Europe, dogs served throughout World War II. (It should be noted that those Alaskan Search and Rescue operations resulted in one hundred crewmen being returned to safety.) If their efforts were hampered by anything, it was the lack of proper training, most of which was due to the fact that the time frame was so restrictive and that there was a relative lack of prior experience in training dogs for warfare. Sometimes Mother Nature intervened to keep dogs from showing their true effectiveness. Several officers within the army's chain of command lobbied hard and long for the use of dogs as haulers during the Battle of the Bulge. The wintry conditions made it difficult for man and machine to do the work of moving materiel and supplies. More than two hundred dogs were trained and dispatched to France and Belgium, but their training time delayed arrival, and the warmer weather, which melted the snow, made them less useful than if they had been able to be deployed immediately.

Similar kinds of shortfalls occurred because dogs were trained by exposing them to small-arms fire but not artillery—again, those lessons of "train like you fight" and expose dogs to every possible environmental stimulus come into play here. Fortunately for someone like me, those mistakes were made and we benefited from them later. While most messenger dogs completed their missions, there are various accounts of dogs being so spooked by the intensity of the sounds of heavy artillery that they didn't make their appointed rounds. In retrospect, it's easy to assign blame for those oversights, but an important point to keep in mind is that we in the United States didn't have extensive experience in using dogs in combat situations. Even those who had, like the British, also made some of the same kinds of mistakes in preparing dogs for warfare operations.

At the conclusion of the fighting in World War II, the QMC continued to be responsible for the canine programs. Because the conflict had ended, most of the dogs were trained and used for sentry duty. In 1951, the QMC was no longer in charge of the MWDs. That responsibility was transferred to the Military Police Corps. This move also signaled the abandonment of scouting and messenger training. First at Fort Riley in Kansas and later at Fort Carson in Colorado, the dogs were trained to serve as guards almost exclusively—a more valuable use in peacetime. While this was going on, the Korean War had started, with some dogs being transferred from sentry duty to combat operations. The Twenty-sixth Infantry Scout Dog Platoon, which had been training in Kansas, was immediately deployed to Korea and eventually earned a citation for its outstanding work in hundreds of missions. The citation identified the particular strengths of the dogs working on point, noted that casualty figures would have been greater had they not been there, and gave particular praise to the handlers and others who earned numerous awards, including Silver Stars and Bronze Stars for valor and meritorious service. After the cessation of fighting and signing of the peace agreement, many canines served by patrolling the newly established demilitarized zone between the two Koreas.

By the time the war in Vietnam began, we realized the various purposes dogs could serve in the military. As a result, dogs engaged in four main activities during that conflict: scouting, tracking, water detection, and sentry work. Water detection isn't what it may sound like. The navy used dogs to detect the presence of human beings in and under the water in order to defend its bases, ships, supplies, and personnel. I should also add that this kind of sentry and detection isn't any less important or dangerous than combat duty. Every branch of the military is proud of its accomplishments and contributions, human and canine, and members of the air force are no different in this regard. Maybe not as well known as Rin Tin Tin or Stubby, the air force MWD Nemo and his contributions are of particular importance.

A German shepherd dog, Nemo, was sent to Tan Son Nhut Air Base to work with his handler among the 377th Security Police Squadron. In December of 1966, the base came under Vietcong attack. Two handlers released their dogs to pursue the enemy, and the dogs were killed in action. The dogs' altering of the presence of the enemy enabled the security forces to kill thirteen guerillas while suffering three casualties among the airmen. Later that same night, Nemo and his handler, Bob Thorneburg, were on patrol near a cemetery adjacent to the air base. They took on enemy fire and both were wounded. Even though Nemo sustained a bullet wound that entered through his right eye and exited his mouth, he continued to pursue the Vietcong, enabling Thorneburg to call in the support of a Quick Reaction Team. Despite his wounds, Nemo crawled back to Thorneburg and covered him with his own body. Though they were still under fire and Thorneburg sustained a second wound, they were extracted from the field. Both eventually recovered.

Nemo returned to the United States and Lackland Air Force Base, the site of the air force's dog-training center, where he lived as a mascot and a recruiter for the program, making personal and televised appearances. His presence at the training center served as a reminder of how important the relationship is between a canine and his handler.

Along with different branches of the military celebrating the exploits of its members, different groups that favor certain breeds also keep alive the memory of their favorites. Combat Tracker Teams (CTTs) also served with distinction in Vietnam, using Labrador retrievers and their especially keen olfactory abilities and their even disposition and adaptability. To be fair, the vast majority of dogs that served in Vietnam were German shepherds. The oppressive heat and humidity of Southeast Asia was one factor that militated against the use of dogs there. The military command was originally highly resistant to the use of dogs there simply due to the weather and the effects it would have on the dogs' performance. A few trials demonstrated that the dogs were more than capable of adapting, and the German shepherd did this (by losing its undercoat) better than most.

As has been well documented, Vietnam presented a new challenge to American fighting forces. The guerilla nature of the warfare, the denseness of the jungle, the scattered site villages all contributed to the notion that the Vietcong were especially elusive. In order to combat this, new tactics needed to be employed. Of course, there's little that is "new" in any war; it becomes a question of adapting and adopting tactics used by others elsewhere. Combat Tracker Teams serve as a good example of this. Adapting training and implementation programs from the British Jungle Warfare School, American military leadership employed Combat Tracking Teams. At first separately, and later together, dog, handler, a team leader, a visual tracker, a radiotelephone operator, and a cover man trained to combat the tactics employed by the Vietcong. They had two main purposes: to make contact with the enemy and to detect any recent enemy activity in the area. Learning jungle craft was critical to feeling at home in an environment that was so foreign to these men and dogs.

The CTT units faced the same issues we do today with our SEAL Team dogs and handlers. They train separately for a while and then the SEAL MWDs and handlers have to integrate themselves into the larger force. Just as is true today, the dogs' natural advantages and skills made that transition easy. With their innate tracking skills honed by additional training, the CTT Labs quickly made the men realize that

while they were called "trackers," they were essentially following the dogs' lead. The men went from thinking *What the
hell is that dog doing here?* to *Why the hell didn't we always have
these dogs?* in a matter of a few hours.

The contributions of the CCT Labrador retrievers and
their handlers didn't receive a great deal of publicity or ac-
claim. In fact, the program was phased out entirely in 1970,
but the lessons learned and the efforts of the dogs have been
kept alive by breed enthusiasts and some participants and
supporters of the program.[11] In addition to their tracking
work, the CCT dogs were also used to locate lost and missing
friendlies. Together with a larger force working in advance of
the CCT troops, the program was a success. Labrador retrievers also worked with the army as part of a tracker team. The
difference between a scout team and tracker team is this:
scouts search an area for signs of an enemy's presence; trackers do the same but also then pursue that enemy aggressively.
In all, nearly a dozen army tracker teams worked in support
of U.S. troops during the Vietnam War. In addition to pursuing human targets, MWDs in Vietnam did what we train our
dogs to do today—to find explosives. That detection work,
complicated by the fact that the Vietcong frequently employed
series of caves and tunnels, once again showed how dogs'
adaptability to foreign environments and their courage and
other attributes could best be used to our advantage.

Estimates vary, but as many as five thousand dogs and ten
thousand handlers served their country from 1964 to 1975.
Accurate accounting practices weren't put in place until 1968,
which explains why this is an estimate rather than a certainty.[12] The sad reality is that, with few exceptions like Nemo,

the vast majority of those dogs didn't return to the United States. The reality of warfare resulted in handlers having to either set their dogs loose to fend for themselves or turn them over to the South Vietnamese army. Either way, it had to be a horrifically painful decision to leave a valued teammate behind.

After Vietnam, this cycle continued—of not being certain of the dogs' effectiveness, learning that they were capable, rushing the training programs, verifying the dogs' usefulness, and employing them in combat and on patrol, and then essentially dismantling the programs and forgetting much of what was learned. It seemed as if during peacetime, little real thought was given to how much dogs had aided us during the various conflicts. We were slow to adopt the idea of using dogs, made some awkward and ill-advised moves, recovered, and benefited, but never fully developed a sustained program of using our canine companions fully in warfare. Dogs returned to their role as sentries—a valuable one, as I've said—but not one that fully utilizes their amazing abilities. Unfortunately, it took another attack on American soil, similar to Pearl Harbor, to resurrect our reliance on dogs in key strategic implementations. September 11, 2001 served as a wake-up call and a rallying cry in many ways.

New York City was, obviously, one site of the attacks that altered the course of our nation. Everyone has their recollections of where they were that day once the news reached them. For me and for my fellow SEALs, as well as for anyone in the military, we quickly realized that the course of our service lives was going to change. I can't say that other teams besides Team 6 wouldn't have begun to use canines if it weren't for 9/11, but certainly that horrible event triggered a need for heightened security on the civilian side and hastened our preparedness for the eventual conflicts our military engaged in.

In a city that was unsettled by the attacks, dogs have played a prominent role in returning the lives of its citizens to a more "normal" level of concern. Interestingly, since 2001, New York City's uniformed police roles have experienced a 17 percent decline in numbers. The number of canine members has doubled. Today, one hundred dogs serve the citizens of New York in either the narcotics, bomb, emergency-response, or transit squads.[13] Even for those of us who don't live in major metropolitan areas, the sight of dogs working at airports and other places is at least familiar as we travel or watch news reports. It may have taken a while for us to get used to the idea that ports of various kinds, from bus stations to major international airports, were patrolled by men with automatic weapons, but we seem to have adjusted fairly easily to the idea of dogs being present in those places.

The Department of Defense has spent nearly twenty million dollars on explosive detection since 2006. Non-canine detection units have had a 50 percent success rate, but the canine units raise that number by another 30 percent. That's a huge increase, and it is little wonder then that the Naval Special Warfare brass came to the same conclusion that New York City and other agencies have: dogs are the best detection "tool" available.

It would take one of my best dogs to "sniff out" the SEALs' previous history of the use of dogs in warfare. Not much is known about how dogs served in Vietnam, so that program remains shrouded in mystery. Whether that's intentional or simply an oversight, or part of the SEAL community's adherence to the "need to know" nature of nearly everything we do, is hard to say. What we do know is this: dogs were used, they were successful in helping operators, and when the war ended, the program was essentially abandoned. That's a pretty familiar scenario, and there are even those who believe that the same thing should be done with the SEAL program entirely in times of peace.

The problem with having the program disbanded is also familiar: when you want to start up a program again, you're basically starting from scratch. In the case of the SEALs' canine program, the problem was even more acute. No active duty member of the teams had been in Vietnam and worked with dogs during that last use of canines in combat. So when the activity in the two most current theaters, Iraq and Afghanistan, intensified and the call went out for a dog program to be created in 2004, this was another case of demand far outstripping supply. What added to this scenario was the fact that municipalities, other branches of the military, other Special Operations Forces, all came to the same conclusion at roughly the same time.

Urgency and expediency won out. Everyone was on the lookout for dogs, and the easiest place from which to source them was within the military itself. After all, patrol dogs and detection dogs were still being used in the regular military. So, because something is better than nothing, these dogs were attached to some SEAL Teams and sent downrange. This is no knock on the work that those trainers and handlers did, but, as I've pointed out before, there is a substantial difference between a MWD and an SOF dog's capabilities and requirements. Also, the handlers who were assigned to these teams weren't up to speed on the kinds of tactical movements that the SEAL Teams employed as a regular part of their repertoire. So, on the one hand, you've got a high-speed, very advanced, tactically charged unit that's trying to shoot, move, and communicate with a guy who has had the responsibilities of a military policeman and hasn't spent the last five years of his life drilling day in and day out with these more advanced tactics.

The fit wasn't the best, and it became clear to everyone involved that a relatively simple equation existed theoretically but was problematic pragmatically: SOF units needed SOF canines. Given that what U.S. Army Rangers do and how they train is different from the SEAL Teams, and that what SEAL Teams do differs from what Green Berets and all the other various special forces do, those who used canines developed their own programs to meet their specific needs. The acquisition, training, and utilization of these dogs has evolved since 9/11, as we've learned more and gained additional experience in the field.

There's no unanimity among trainers, breeders, or handlers on all issues, but everyone agrees that as detection tools, dog exceed any machine's capabilities. Numerous groups have tried to build machines that replicate what a dog does. To this point, for a variety of reasons, the machines haven't been able to surpass that 80 percent success rate canines provide. In addition, they haven't been cost-effective enough, or had other problems, so using them to replace dogs entirely in serving in this important capacity is unwise and hasn't happened.

As with most things regarding SEAL Teams and any additions to the program, be it technology, tactics, and so on, SEAL Team 6 pioneered the way with their canine program. They created and refined the program, the training procedures, and other elements of working with SOF canines trickled down to the teams on the East and West Coasts. As I was leaving the navy, the canine program was starting to go into a higher gear in and around Coronado. I'd already purchased property and had plans already in place to create the best dog-training facility I could. My connections within the SOF community certainly helped me get my business started, and I'm grateful for that. The truth is, though, that if I weren't able to provide them with dogs that succeeded downrange, I wouldn't continue to get contracts to do what I do. I'm also grateful that I can contribute to our ongoing efforts in however indirect a manner as I presently do. I felt that there was a need for someone like me to be out here in civilian life to help meet the need for these highly skilled multi-purpose dogs.

Those of us who train SOF canines are a very small and very tight-knit community. We assist one another in every way we can. We sometimes trade dogs among ourselves when the need arises. There's no room for us to let egos or dollars get in the way of succeeding at job one—training dogs that will save our brothers' lives.

Like me, Aaron grew up knowing what he wanted to do with his life. Living in South Dakota, just outside Rapid City, he couldn't see Mount Rushmore, but he had a living, breathing example of our country's greatness near at hand. His grandfather was a member of the Greatest Generation, and, like mine and so many others, he didn't sit around spinning yarns about his exploits. No one else in Aaron's family seemed to place much emphasis on Grandpa Jim's experiences, but as Aaron said, "I was just extremely interested. There was something about the military that I liked, so I started asking him about World War Two. And once he started talking, he opened up and just told me all kinds of amazing stories."

Aaron's grandfather was a boatswain's mate on three different ships and was one of those patriotic Americans who enlisted the day after Pearl Harbor. He was also one of those fortunate Americans who served for the duration, including a lengthy stint aboard the USS *Portland,* which saw duty in major naval battles in the Pacific. From Guadalcanal to Corregidor to Okinawa, the men aboard the USS *Portland* served with distinction. Aaron's grandfather didn't glorify the war for him, and Aaron recalled some of the horrific elements of naval combat, but mostly he remembered what his grandfather told him about the camaraderie among the crewmen and the lifelong friendships he made.

"Basically, he said that those experiences were the best and worst times of his life."

Aaron described himself as a rambunctious, semidelinquent kind of kid who frequently found himself in trouble. That lead to his desire to join the military. "I wanted to be sneaky, and I thought Special Operations were cool." He'd heard about the marine's Force Reconnaissance from a neighbor who was a part of that group. His plans to join the marines changed when a friend's brother returned from the United States Naval Academy over the Christmas holidays. Aaron had never heard of the SEALs, but he began to research, and from the age of thirteen on, he knew that he one day wanted to belong to those elite teams. He told himself that as soon as he graduated from high school, he was going to join the navy.

"I was big into swimming. I loved doing martial arts, so as soon as I read about the Navy SEALs, that was it."

As much as he liked swimming, Aaron wasn't on the swim team, but he did play water polo. "Play" isn't exactly the right word. "Because I didn't have the cardio fitness of the other guys and couldn't even complete all the practice laps, the coaches just told me to go into the other pool while the other guys practiced and scrimmaged. I kind of realized I was a terrible swimmer." Eventually Aaron overcame that, but it took some time and a lot of hard work.

"I'm a big reader, and I love to research things before I get into them, so I knew what I was getting into. I researched the hell out of the decision to become a SEAL Team member. But I really underestimated how hard it was going to be. When I showed up for BUD/S training, I wasn't ready. Out of a class of one hundred and eighty-six or so guys, I was the second slowest runner in the class. After the first day, the slowest guy quit, so I became *the* slowest."

Aaron can laugh about the situation now, but at the time, it took all his mental strength to get through it. He'd enlisted at the tail end of 1993 and then spent nearly three years training to become and then serving as a corpsman before graduating from BUD/S in 1997. As a member of his SEAL Team, he served initially in the PACOM (Pacific Command) theater out of Guam. "We traveled a lot doing Foreign Internal Defense (FID) and training other countries' Special Ops guys. I was in Thailand, Malaysia, Singapore, Australia, the Philippines."

In 2004, on his third deployment to Iraq, he was doing Direct Action Missions, hunting down high-value targets there. Later, like me, he transitioned from chasing bad guys to protecting good guys, serving on a personal security detail for members of the interim government. After this fourth platoon deployment, he was assigned shore duty for one year. That didn't sit well with him. "I had a desk job working with the medical department. I basically was responsible for assigning other corpsman to be on hand when the SEALs were doing training exercises. If a SEAL platoon went to the range to shoot, they needed a medic there. I was the guy who sent a non-SEAL corpsman to those locations."

Aaron wasn't happy being a desk jockey, but orders were orders. One day in 2006, he was asked to send a corpsman to accompany a SEAL Team doing dog training. Aaron sent one, but his curiosity was piqued. "Even before our guy came back and told me about how awesome it was to see what they were doing with these dogs, I was asking questions when the request came in. After he told me about it, I had to see this for myself."

The next time a corpsman was needed, Aaron tagged along for a day to watch the canine training. He watched the handlers working the dogs on explosive-detection scenarios and came away impressed with the dogs' capabilities. Later, watching bite-work exercises, he was even more impressed. He'd heard about MWDs and seen a few in Iraq during his four deployments there, but seeing them up close made a major impression on him.

"I'd worked briefly in Iraq with dogs from conventional forces—marines and army—but basically we told their handlers how things were going to go: *We're going to go hit some house, and if a bad guy runs out the back, you send the dog after him.* That was the limit of my interaction with dogs to that point. After seeing those training exercises, I realized there was a lot they could do."

He found out from the OIC that they were looking for volunteers. Aaron asked the question that every military man considering volunteering for a program would: "What's the catch?"

He was told there was none. He would have to make a two-year commitment at minimum. He'd be given a dog, be trained as a handler himself, and then he would get to deploy.

"That was the magic word. This was still wartime, and the dogs were guaranteed to deploy to the hottest spots because, obviously, that's where they were needed the most."

Aaron wanted to make certain he had things clear in his mind, "So I said to the OIC, 'So you're telling me if I come over here right now, you're going to give me a dog and I'm going to get to go to combat?' When he said yes, I said, 'Oh, shit yeah, I'm there.'"

By 2007, Aaron was among the first handlers, outside of SEAL Team 6 on the East Coast, to be working with dogs. The program was so new at the time that, as Aaron put it, "You could have asked any SEAL if there's a dog team, and most would have said no. A few would have said, 'We don't, but Team Six does.' Basically, we existed before anyone outside our group knew we existed."

Fortunately for Aaron, and for the dog-team members, he was a corpsman by training. That likely contributed to his transfer request being approved, and he served double duty as the corpsman and handler. His medical duties also included caring for the dogs, and he served as a kind of veterinary technician for them. Eventually, he took as many courses in canine medicine that he could to get up to speed.

Not everything Aaron had been told by the OIC proved true, but that was okay. The program was in its infancy but well funded. Along with other members of the team, Aaron got to travel to Germany and Holland to observe the basic training regimens the dogs underwent. Aaron needed that kind of exposure since he had never worked with dogs. His family kept dogs as pets, but he wasn't what he'd consider "a dog guy." After the first few months of training, he was hooked. "I fell in love with it. This was the best time in my career."

Part of that had to do with being liberated from a desk job, but a lot of it had to do with his interactions with his dog, Castor. Aaron laughingly talks about Castor being a first-round draft pick. At the time, the Special Operations Command realized that there was a great need for dogs all across the Special Operations Forces spectrum. Vendors were found who could supply dogs, and then representatives of the Green Berets, MARSOF (Maritime Special Operations Forces), the SEAL Teams, and the Rangers all went on site to view and select the dogs. At each "draft" camp, one group would be given the first pick, and then at a later one, another group would get the first selection, and so on. Aaron knew going in that the West Coast teams had the first pick. Before the skills demonstration began, they got to view the candidates.

"It was an extremely tight-quarters kennel, and the smell was horrendous. The sound level was ridiculous as well. We were all walking through there, and some of the dogs were barking, some were spinning tight circles, and just about every one of them was going nuts in some way. Then I saw Castor. He was sitting there, staring back at this group of strangers staring at him. He was just chilling, and nothing fazed him at all. I called him over so that I could pet him, but he just kept staring at me like, *Yeah, whatever; I'm not doing that.* So I bent down and looked at him, and I knew he was the one. I liked his calm demeanor. I'm a pretty calm guy, and pairing him with someone like me had a lot of appeal. I told myself I was going to keep my eye on this one."

During the selection and bite work, Castor stood out. Later, when talking with trainers/vendors, they confirmed that Castor had great skills. The rest of the Special Operations guys seemed dubious.

"We were all relatively new at this and didn't have a lot of experience with training dogs and none with working in the field with them. Most of the other guys wanted one of those really big and aggressive types that had been so disruptive in the kennel. What convinced me that Castor was the right one was when we got to do some early socialization work with them."

For this part of the selection process, Castor was muzzled and led out of his kennel. Aaron got Castor to lie down and then joined him on the ground. He'd hop over his back and then wrap his arms around him. The point was to see what kind of human aggression the dog would demonstrate toward a handler. Castor took it all in stride. Aaron also picked Castor up, something that makes even the mildest of dogs edgy, but again, Castor showed no discomfort.

"A lot of these dogs, you touch them and they want to eat your ass. They're just angry animals. But Castor was like, *Yep. Just another day.* I knew this dog was perfect for me because he was a superstar in the drills and he was completely social."

Though Aaron wasn't an experienced dog trainer, he innately understood the point I'd made about how important the bond of trust is between a dog and his handler. That Castor allowed himself to be touched and picked up without complaint meant that he'd adapt easily to working with a new person and that the basic level of trust of humans was already in place. Castor sensed that this person wasn't going to hurt him. That trait demonstrated itself later during helicopter training in preparation for fast-roping insertions.

Aaron had strapped Castor into his tactical vest, which is equipped with a handle at its top. To expose the dog to that environment takes some time. Initially, just getting a dog used to the sound of the engines and the wind-whipped air is enough. Eventually, though, you have to get the dog in the helo and off the ground. Most dogs are resistant to not having all four paws firmly planted on the ground, so you can imagine how difficult it would be to get a dog to climb out of a helicopter's bay into thin air. Aaron and the other early handler trainees employed a sink-or-swim approach.

"I had to take Castor and grab the handle of his vest, lift him up, and then dangle him out over the lip of the helicopter. He thought I was throwing him out of the bird, and he freaked out—paws thrashing, his torso twisting. Once I let go of him, and of course he's tethered to me, he dropped a couple of inches more and then just hung there. He was immediately totally calm, and I imagined he was thinking, *Oh, okay, cool. This is fine. Dad's got me.*"

That kind of trust is essential to the relationship between a MWD and his handler. Castor and Aaron had it from the outset, and that bond only hardened as time went on. Much of that was due to Aaron's dedication. Though admittedly not a dog person and someone who saw the SEAL Team's use of dogs as a way out of a desk job and back into combat, Aaron put the research and reading skills that he had utilized in making the decision to enter the navy and the SEAL program to use in working with dogs. Unlike some of his fellow SEAL handlers, Aaron was an early convert to operant conditioning, partly based on his research and partly on his relationship with Castor. "He was my friend. I didn't want to have to correct him. I didn't want to have to jerk him around. If I could make him more receptive and get better results without all those negative punishments, then, even though I was going against the grain, nobody could say anything against me. To me, it wasn't enough to go through the handler program and get dogs to do their jobs. I wanted to know how they thought, how they learned, and what I could get him to do without inflicting pain on him."

Aaron took the same approach to his job as a dog handler as he did with everything else in his career as a SEAL. He knew that the job the dogs would eventually do was too important for him not to learn as much as he possibly could. At that point in the early development of the program, those training the handlers only had fairly limited experience with old-school methods of training and disciplining dogs. Aaron was concerned that those methods might have their limits.

"I want to be the best at every single thing I do. I also have a lot of natural curiosity, so I wanted to learn as much as I could. More important, if I show up in Afghanistan or wherever with my dog, and I introduce myself to the unit I'm assigned to, I have a great deal of responsibility on my shoulders. If that dog accidentally bites one of my guys, or if that dog doesn't detect some explosives and guys get wounded or killed, that's on me. That's my fault, not the dog's. And what if that guy who got bit has to be sent home, and then his replacement comes along and something happens to him?"

The downside of having that kind of bond with a dog, if there is one at all, may be in what Aaron felt as additional pressure—not just for his fellow soldiers, but with the dog that he'd come to care so much about.

"When you're walking point with your dog, you're the first one to see bad guys. If anything happens to anyone else, it's your fault. That's a lot of pressure to carry around. Even so, when I'm out walking point and I've got my dog in front of me looking for explosives, I'm also worried about his well-being. When you're doing that detection work, your sole focus is on wind direction. If you're patrolling down a trail and there's only one way to enter this trail that is tactically sound, and if you're unlucky enough that on that particular night the wind is at your back and not pushing those odors toward you, the stress gets even more intense. Castor could step on a pressure plate even before he smelled those explosives, just as easily as a human could—some of those antipersonnel pressure plates are that sensitive. The thought of getting that dog hurt, because he trusted me enough to go there, added to the burden. We love each other. I can honestly say that if Castor got injured, I would have as hard a time dealing with that as I would if something happened to other team members."

Part of the reason why Castor and Aaron bonded is due to the qualities that dog possessed. On a training exercise, Castor and Aaron were moving through a heavily wooded area. They were patrolling along a road during this bite-work exercise, when Castor came on human odor. Aaron released him, and Castor ripped through the woods in pursuit. Aaron watched as Castor leapt through some brush and then disappeared. Eventually Aaron caught up to the trainer in the bite suit, fully engaged with the dog near a rocky outcropping. Blood spattered the gray stone. Aaron began calling for Castor to release, fearful that the dog had punctured both the bite suit and the human underneath it. Instead, what he saw was blood gushing out of his dog's chest. On closer examination, he could see that Castor had impaled himself on a sharp stick. It entered his body with such force that the stick was still underneath his skin, extending down from the entry point on his chest and down his flank for about twelve inches. As horrified as he was, Aaron was also impressed that a wound that severe hadn't slowed Castor down a bit.

Regulations required the dogs to be kept on site, so in order to treat Castor, Aaron had to drive home to get additional equipment he kept there. He also brought his wife back to serve as a surgical nurse. In the field, Aaron had removed most of the stick, but he could feel that more was still buried beneath his skin and fur. Castor didn't show great signs of distress, so Aaron didn't anesthetize him. Even without a muzzle on the dog, Aaron and his wife felt safe performing minor surgery on the dog—removing the remaining pieces of stick and flushing the wound with various antiseptics. Following that and a few sutures, Castor was out of commission for only a week. Obviously, not every handler can provide their dog with that kind of medical treatment, but as I pointed out earlier, letting your dog know that you provide for his needs is an essential step in building that all-important bond of trust.

In ways large and small, Aaron did that, and he was rewarded with a dog whose performance in the field was outstanding. Aaron also went above and beyond some of the
training standards of those early days and had Castor laser
trained. One of the skills that dogs possess is their ability to
follow nonverbal commands—hand signals, for example—
but they are also capable of following our gaze. If we first
engage the dog to get its attention and then look elsewhere,
the dog will look where we look. In the field, that has limited
applications, but getting a dog to follow a laser pointer's red
dot is especially useful. The SEAL Teams also have a pointer
that is not visible to the naked eye but can be viewed through
our night-vision goggles. Castor was trained on the visible
type, utilizing this "look where I look" capability.

In the field then, Aaron could get Castor's attention, show
him the laser apparatus, and then point the beam into a specific area, and Castor would go to that point. When on the bite
command, for example, Aaron could have multiple targets in
front of him and use the laser to tell which of the ten people
in front of him is the one that Castor should apprehend. Ad-
ditionally, Aaron could target with the laser a particular door
or wall among a series of them and direct Castor to that area.
Again, keep in mind that this could be done either in full
daylight or in pitch blackness, and from a distance of two
hundred to three hundred yards. Once Castor has the *sook*
command to find an object and is off-leash, he will go immediately to that specific area.

That's a particularly effective clearing method that would
then allow the team members to place ladders against those

walls to climb over, or to place a breaching charge to blow a door without worrying about an IED being present.

Aaron also pushed Castor's apprehension training to the point that he felt 100 percent confident that his dog would not bite anyone dressed similarly to his handler—unless instructed to. That was especially important because frequently when on a mission, Castor would enter an area after having been given the *reviere* command, in other words, to apprehend or bite someone. Given the confusion of numerous people being in a confined space, friendlies and others, a less-disciplined dog might take on anyone regardless. Aaron is convinced of and has seen evidence of Castor's ability to identify friend from foe. On numerous patrols in Afghanistan, in crowded bazaars, in homes, and in open areas, Castor has learned to sort through the individuals there, running through the legs or past one person in pursuit of the bad guy.

Much time and effort was spent in helping the dogs learn good guys from bad guys. Since dogs learn by association and repetition, we have to create scenarios similar to what they will encounter in the field. During apprehension work the dogs would be unleashed and sent into a compound on the *reviere* command. One instructor would be in a bite suit, while other trainees would act as the members of an assault team who would follow the dog into that area. If the dog went after one of the assaulters, who was dressed just like the handler so that the association was clear, he'd be corrected. Repeat that enough and the dog gets it that those who are dressed like "my dad" (we frequently use that term to describe the handler to reinforce the idea that the bond of trust between human and canine is so important) are okay and anyone else isn't.

While all dogs are capable of learning this distinction, that doesn't mean that we want to put it to use. As Aaron said to me, "You can have an extremely good working dog, but some of them just don't have that kind of demeanor. Some of them are just too reactive. They're like that guy in the bar who no matter what you say to him will be itching for a brawl. Some dogs seem to believe that *Since you gave me the command to bite, then damn it, that's what I'm going to do.* Those kinds of dogs can be especially difficult to work with in a large group. Castor was not one of those.

Aaron and Castor worked together on two deployments in Afghanistan, doing much the same kind of work as Rocket, detecting explosives primarily. The two were able to utilize the tools they learned in training to clear buildings and provide protection for the troops they served with.

In some ways Aaron and Castor's story is unique. Each of their individual attributes meshed well together. They were there at the beginning of the program, before I began providing and training dogs for the teams. They serve as a template for the kind of heart and mind that is necessary to take on the task of being the tip of the spear. Aaron's dedication to the program and to his dog differ only slightly from the devotion that most pet owners feel toward the four-legged friend in their lives.

I don't have to check on Castor now that he's retired from active duty. Aaron is now a trainer at BUD/S, and Castor lives with Aaron and his family. While I sat and talked with Aaron, Castor lay at his feet, waiting. Aaron told me that as soon as we were finished up, he was going to go to work and Castor was going to accompany him. That day's training activities for the next class of SEALs involved some beach running. Castor liked that. Other days, Castor can be found at Aaron's wife's office. He's taken over a couch there, and he's content to watch her typing away at her computer. Once the tapping sounds end, he looks at her and she at him. It's lunchtime or break time, and that means a walk around the area. A tennis ball is frequently involved. At quitting time, the two head home, and then Castor hangs out there with both his mom and his dad. He's seldom alone, and Aaron and his wife take him just about everywhere they go. He's adjusted well to his downtime and is about as content as any dog can be in knowing that he's well cared for and respected for what he's done for one man and one woman and for their, and his, country.

The old saying goes, "Curiosity killed the cat." Well, in the case of one Navy SEAL working dog, a serviceman's overly curious nature really pissed off a multi-purpose K9 named Samson. According to his handler, SEAL Team 3 member Dave, the first time he met with the platoon he was assigned to in Kandahar, Afghanistan, he did what he'd been trained to do. He introduced himself and his Malinois Samson to the assembled group of battle-tested frogmen. He began by asking how many of these men had served in a unit that was accompanied by a MWD. Just a few hands went up, and when questioned further, they revealed that the only dogs they'd seen had been sentry dogs back in the United States. That wasn't surprising. In 2009, according to a resolution submitted in the House Committee on Armed Services, a total of two thousand MWDs served at nearly 170 United States military bases worldwide, including those in forty states and three U.S. territories.[1] That the resolution did not mention the number of MWDs serving in Iraq and Afghanistan, though they were mentioned generally, isn't surprising. Revealing troop strength figures isn't a common military practice, whether or not those numbers reflect animals or humans.

The House resolution was submitted in honor of MWD Ben CO20, an air force sentry dog that was retiring after eleven years of service. This reflects the military's growing recognition of the importance of canines in the post–9/11 security world. No less an authority than CIA Director and Four-Star General David Petraeus recognized their value when he said of MWDs, "The capability they bring to the fight cannot be replicated by man or machine."[2] I'm not sure that one of Samson's capabilities was what General Petraeus had in mind when he made that statement.

After PO3 Dave finished his introductory remarks, he asked the members of the platoon to form a circle. He wanted them to each get a chance to handle Samson. This was designed to let them get comfortable with the dog and vice versa. He gave a detailed explanation of how the handoffs would go. He would bend down and pick up Samson, careful to wrap him up tightly and to secure all four of his legs. Only then would he hand the dog off to the next person in line. That person would hold the dog for a few moments. Dave reminded them that it was important that he take Samson back and then only he would hand the dog off to the next person in the line. That was his way of communicating to Samson that this was all okay. He was telling him in a sense that if Dad was handing you over to someone, then you have to trust that new person, because I do.

Things went according to plan until an overeager soldier forgot about the handler-first rule. As soon as Samson was back on the ground, and still in Dave's control, this guy bent down, put his face right next to Samson's, and tried to hug the dog to his chest in order to lift him up. Fortunately for everyone, Samson was on his best behavior. Instead of biting, he emitted a deeply guttural growl that let the solider know that Samson didn't appreciate him not following orders.

As Dave later told me, "That guy got off on the wrong foot with Samson, and he never forgot that breach of etiquette. Samson wasn't properly introduced to him, the guy overstepped his bounds, and from that point forward, whenever Samson saw the guy, he would growl." Worse, the soldier in question professed to being a dog lover and was extremely interested in Samson and Dave and the training they'd undergone and other elements of the dog's life. Dave had to do his best to integrate himself into this group, and he didn't want to be rude. Also, he'd told the guys that if they ever had any questions, he'd be happy to answer them. He just didn't anticipate how many questions this one team member would have.

After a few days of Samson getting to know everyone and adjusting to his new home, he wasn't always on leash while on the grounds of the FOB. Samson was gregarious enough that he didn't pose a biting threat. He proved to be a popular presence, and in a few weeks, both he and Dave seemed to have meshed well with the unit.

Several days after being attached to the team, Samson and Dave got word that they would be going out on a mission with the platoon. All the guys, including Dave, prepared early and left their gear outside where they were billeted. They'd suit up at the last minute after their final briefings, taking care of whatever personal business they had, and so on. Dave recalls walking out into a central area where piles of gear dotted the compound. He released Samson, who went to work immediately, nose to the ground, tail in the air, trying to locate any snacks. Or at least that was what Dave thought. Samson went from pile to pile and finally settled on one rucksack.

He looked around, almost as if checking to see if anyone was looking. Then he lifted his leg and let out a nice stream of golden piss on that pile. Dave felt bad, but what could he do? He stood on the side waiting to see who the lucky one was. You've probably already figured out who that individual was, and you're right. The impatient operator won the honor that Samson had bestowed on him. Dave isn't a malicious guy, but he had to laugh at his buddy Samson and his way of getting his revenge. Another saying comes to mind: "Payback is a bitch." In this case though, it wasn't. It came in the form of that same male black-and-tan Malinois with an oversized head, named Samson.

It was the difference in color and size between Samson's head and body that first caught Dave's attention when the two of them first met one another. Samson was small framed, with a camel-colored torso and hindquarters, but with a coal-black head and snout that, in certain light, hid his liquid, expressive eyes. Dave admitted that this was not a case of love at first sight. "I'd seen all the other dogs, and then when he was assigned to me, I thought, *What the hell? Why was I the one getting a dog that looked like it had been Frankenstein-ed together from two other dogs?* He was smaller than the dogs the rest of the guys in my training group were assigned, and that big head of his made him look like a buffalo or something. That image stuck, and eventually we all at one time or another thought of my big-skulled guy as Buffalo Head."

Dave's words sound harsher than they were. When we talked about him, there was obvious deep affection between the two of them. Dave was no longer working with Samson after two years serving several stints together in Afghanistan.

"Samson has one more deployment scheduled. He has to pass a physical before he can go, and I hate to say this, but I hope he doesn't pass. Not that I want there to be something wrong with him, but I miss being with him. His new handler's a great guy, but Samson and I went through a lot together." Dave's voice trails off, and I can tell that man and dog's enforced absence doesn't sit well with the human part of the team.

I ask Dave about the last time he saw Samson. "You know, I had to be strong when we said good-bye. I couldn't get too worked up about it because of my wife and kids. If they saw me all down, then they would be even more upset. As it was, my wife was kind of torn up about it. He remembers me, though, of course, and the last time I went to visit him, he did his thing with me."

Dave described how Samson's ears pricked up as soon as he saw Dave. He then trotted toward him and thrust his head between Dave's legs so that his buddy could scratch him behind his ears. "Some dogs do that thing—press their head up against you or between your legs. It's so cool that he does that. It's a very expressive gesture. It's like he's telling me that he's home. This is where he belongs. I asked some of the handlers and our trainers about that. They told me that was his way of signaling that he knows that I've got his back and he's got mine. I've got kids, and I equate what Samson does with them coming up to me while I'm watching TV and hugging me or snuggling up against me. It's a very comforting feeling."

Dave knows that Samson is beginning to show some signs of wear and tear after fairly intensive deployments. He's having digestive issues; Dave thinks they're signs of stress, and he worries about what might happen to Samson if he has to go back to Afghanistan one more time. "The dogs get it. They like to work, but humans who are stressed out also surround them. They pick up on that and it affects them. Just like I was saying before about the connection between kids and dogs and those signs of affection. If your house is a stressed-up place, even though you think you're doing your best to hide it, the kids sense it. So do the dogs when out in the field. The work is dangerous, and they do a great job when they're at it, but they have very little downtime."

Dave is eager for Samson to finish up his tests and either get deployed or retire. Either way—wait or not—Dave plans to adopt Samson and give him a good life when the dog finally retires.

So how did these two manage to develop that deep bond when Dave was originally so skeptical? On a variation of another cliché, you can't judge a dog by the markings of his fur or the size of his head.

In some ways, Dave and Samson shared some qualities. It would be easy to look at Dave's past and assume that he was a less-than-ideal candidate for the SEALs if you solely looked at the what and not the why. Born in Brooklyn, New York, the son of a man who ran a small cleaning business that catered to local businesses and offices, Dave didn't have the luxury of exploring his avid interest in sports—cross-country and baseball, in particular. Shortly before he turned twelve years old, his mother left the family. Dave not only lost a mother and her potentially positive influence and guidance, he, his siblings, and his father lost a key source of income. As a result, Dave had to leave school in 1987 at the age of fifteen to work, first with his father and later at a variety of other jobs. Dave liked school, and while he wasn't an outstanding student, his natural curiosity and sharp mind helped him do well. He easily earned his GED, but work took precedence over everything else in his life.

"My dad had to work twenty-four/seven to support us. That's just how it was. You do what you have to do. He had mouths to feed, but he couldn't do it on his own. I was the youngest, so I was the least far along in life—that's one way to put it. My older siblings, a brother and two sisters, were already pretty set on their life paths when my mom left. They had to work hard, too, but they all got through high school, and each of them did some college work. That didn't seem like an option for me."

In the spirit of doing whatever it takes, Dave took a series of jobs for which he wouldn't have been eligible based on his age. Driven to succeed, he altered his brother's driver's license to get a job at a pizza chain store in Brooklyn. Within a year, at the age of seventeen, he was promoted to assistant manager. The work wasn't the most rewarding or challenging, but the money helped. Dave had dreams back then. They mostly revolved around muscle cars—a 1969 Nova, a 1971 Camaro, which he worked on as a shade-tree mechanic—not an easy thing to do in Brooklyn. The streets held another allure besides fast cars. Street gangs, drugs, and petty crime influenced many of Dave's peers. A few were hard-core, but most were just directionless kids with no real idea where they wanted to go or who they wanted to be. Dave put himself in that category, though his work ethic kept him from ever sliding too far down into anything like the serious thug life.

By the time he was twenty, he realized that a career in the fast-food world was, if not a dead end, then at least a long drive down a boring stretch of highway that lead to no place interesting. He enrolled in community college, took a few courses, attended for a bit, and then lost interest. The pattern repeated itself a few times. He found himself always drifting back toward the street life, what was easiest.

A friend told him that he should consider life in the military as a way out. Having a brother who served and seeing little in the way of options based on what he'd seen of his friends and peers on the street, Dave's curiosity was piqued. Not so much that he'd actually do anything serious about it, but he started to do some reading and some talking to guys in the neighborhood. "One guy would say it was a great idea, another would tell me that I was crazy."

The friend who originally planted the seed called him another time and told him about the Navy SEALs. "He said that these guys did the stuff that I was into, only it was legal. He was joking, but when I checked things out, I saw there was some truth to what he was saying."

More than that, Dave realized that making the SEAL Teams would be a real challenge. "Just scraping by trying to make a living was a challenge. I was up to that, and had been for a while. I needed a change."

He was also up for a challenge. He'd spent most of his young adult life trying to escape the idea of being the "baby brother." He wanted to make that transition from being a kid to being a man. About the most seriously illegal thing he'd done was getting a job using a fake ID, but he saw that as a positive. He found a way to get a mission accomplished. He figured that attitude would serve him well. One day he headed over to a local recruitment office.

"I walked in the place, and the first office was for the marines. I'd started to have some doubts about the SEALs. They were the elite and all, and I wondered if I could cut it. So, I walked toward the open door, and this staff sergeant looked me up and down, and this weird kind of smile passed over his face. Then he got serious for a second and yelled out, 'Halt! Stop where you're at. I want you to do an about-face.'

"I stood there staring at the guy, wondering, *What is this guy talking about, about-face?* Before I could say anything, he walked out of this office, saying, again in this loud shrill voice, 'Think about the rest of your life, and then come back in here.'

"I said to him, 'What? Excuse me?'

"'You heard me. Turn around. Get out of here. Think about what you're about to do, and then come back.'

"I stood there shaking my head, trying to figure out what this guy's deal was. Out of the corner of my eye, I saw two other men in uniform. They were seated at desks, and a glass partition separated them from this marine and me. They were both smiling and laughing a bit, and the navy recruiter stood up and walked over to his door and stuck out his head. 'Dude, why don't you come on in here?' "

He sounded like somebody Dave could better relate to, so he went in, and after a couple of introductory exchanges, Dave mentioned his interest in the Navy SEALs. He was handed a brochure, shown a brief video, and that was all it took.

"Sign me up," Dave told the recruiter.

Unfortunately he didn't sign Dave up for the Dive Farer program. Dive Farer was a way for the navy to identify potential candidates for the SEAL teams. They do additional training beyond what the rest of the recruits do. Dave assumed that when he got to boot camp, he'd be with the Dive Farer candidates. When the group was to formally muster, his name wasn't called. Dave went to his basic-training instructor and asked about the omission. There's that old saying about recruiters "getting" guys, and this was one of those cases.

The instructor looked at his list and then at Dave. "Let me guess," he said, "your recruiter told you were going to be a SEAL?"

Dave nodded.

The recruiter shook his head. "No. He got you. You're going to a big old gray ship when you're done here."

Following basic training in 1992, the future SEAL Team

member was assigned a Machine Repairman (MR) rate and put to work. At first he was looking for a way to get out, but he was told that he'd made a four-year commitment. Dave decided that he was going to have to learn to live with his situation. He also learned that no tricks had been played on him. The recruiter had said that he could qualify for the SEALs; Dave had passed the initial physical fitness qualifier, but he hadn't scored high enough on a written test to make the first cut.

In high school, before he'd dropped out, he'd taken the Armed Services Vocational Aptitude Battery (ASVAB) test. His score had been his undoing.

"After scoring so low on that exam was another time when I could only do what I knew best—work my ass off to prove that I could get things done." He proved to be a hustler in the most positive sense. "Being an engineman wasn't my idea of making it to the top and proving myself. I figured that if I had to do my time, I'd take full advantage of every opportunity I had."

That attitude translated into him taking as many courses as he could, earning citations for exemplary work, and doing everything he could to stand out, in a positive way, from the rest of his shipmates. He picked his spots, but he let his superiors know that he was still interested in going into BUD/S training. His plan worked. When told that if he made the next rank, he'd get his shot, he made sure that it happened. It took three years to get into BUD/S, and when he did, he made the most of that chance.

Only later, when he started to work with Samson, did Dave realize that the two of them had been prejudged. Dave,

first by that marine recruiter who took him for a typical kid
off the street (Dave admits that maybe his *Hey, bro, what's up?*
attitude sent the wrong signal), and later Samson, when the
striking contrast between his slight frame and his oversized
head made him appear to be a less-than-ideal candidate. Actually, Samson's head was a slight advantage. If you remember the study done on dog's skulls to determine bite strength,
the longer the lever (jaw) and the broader the skull, the
greater the pressure a dog could exert.

Shortly after working with Samson, Dave discovered that
advantage when the decoys reported back on the tenacity of
the dog's grip. He could hold on, and so could Dave. Prior
to entering the canine program to become a handler, Dave
served for a total of thirteen years, deployed to both Iraq and
Afghanistan. Like most of the other handlers, he'd had expo-
sures to dogs as pets and had seen them work with other
handlers as MWDs before becoming a handler. Some of his
perceptions about Samson were shaped by his childhood
experiences with Rottweilers.

With his father working many hours, and Dave being the
youngest, Dave was frequently left at home alone. For companionship, nothing beat having a dog to come home to from
school. Dave's family had a series of dogs, but the ones he remembers most fondly were the rottweilers they had while
his parents were at work. Coming home from school to a
dog's greeting helped to ease some of the pain he felt at his
mother's departure. The dog was often an escape of sorts for
him. He would take the dog for long walks, and though he
had no real idea of how to formally train a dog, he made his
efforts at it. From the beginning, he paid close attention to

his dog, and he learned from it. He was able to identify that the dogs had different barks in different situations. For example, he was eventually able to identify when the dogs barked whether a stranger was coming to the door or a family member was approaching. Dave laughed when he told me how that ability came in handy: when he and his siblings were doing something they shouldn't have been, the dog served as an early warning device that they had to stop and clean up their act before Mom or Dad came through the door.

With the other dogs, he saw them as the younger siblings that he didn't have. When his human siblings left, and especially after his mother left, the dogs helped to fill the void he felt from their absence. One dog in particular, Rebecca von Hufning, a female rottie, played that role particularly well.

Dave became such a regular in the neighborhood walking his dog that at one point, he was out exercising the dog when a man approached him with another rottweiler. The man was about to go to prison, and he wanted to be sure that his beloved dog would be well cared for. He offered Dave the dog, and Dave accepted. His father wasn't too pleased with idea of having another canine mouth to feed and sometimes used the threat of expelling the dogs from the house to get Dave to do what was asked of him. Father and son had some tension between them, but the threat was never made real. Dave knew that both his father and he relied on the dogs too much to have them be sent away.

Because of Dave's love of dogs, he was an ideal candidate to become a SEAL Team dog handler. Every handler has different motivations for volunteering, and not all of them share Dave's affection for dogs. They admire and respect what they can do, but for some of them, one of the key training mantras we have—"Watch your dog every minute so that you know him better than you've known anybody"—isn't always easy for them to apply. With Dave, that wasn't the case. One of the reasons why we want handlers to be so familiar with all the dog's traits, habits, and even its body has to do with monitoring the dog's mental and physical well-being. As much as we try to re-create realistic battle/operations scenarios, with our SEALs and with their canines, how they might respond when in theater may be different.

A handler has to be able to detect when a dog is not at his best, has been worked too hard, or has developed some negative association with some phase of an operation. If a dog is not working to full capacity, that's like a soldier being distracted by events back home, like a weapon that hasn't been maintained properly and might misfire, or a piece of communications or other equipment that has either been overused or somehow damaged. All those things become a liability. When Dave talked about the stress that he felt, he was talking about this aspect of the canine-human pairing. The dog, because he doesn't have the ability to speak our language, can't "tell" you when he's not at his best. He can't do that in words, but there are other "tells," like a poker player who scratches his ear in order to appear casual but his opponents realize it reveals that he is bluffing.

An important thing to remember about these dogs is that because they are bred and trained at such a high level, like any supremely competitive athlete, they want to be in the game all the time despite how they feel. The signs of a dog's not performing 100 percent are often subtle. The years spent in training and the developing of the bond between handler and canine help to familiarize the human with dog so that he can better spot those minor fluctuations. Dave was a keen observer, and he recognized very quickly some of Samson's behaviors that helped him figure out what his dog was thinking and feeling. Early on, he noticed how Samson interacted with other dogs, particularly ones that he didn't like. "If he doesn't like a dog, he'll shake his tail—wave it back and forth three or four times and stop, then three or four times and stop, three or four times and stop. He's almost luring the dog in, because when they wag their tails, they're letting the other dog know that they're friendly and that everything's okay. He was kind of disguising his real intentions."

Anyone who's ever owned a dog knows that they are "creatures of habit." Put another way, they exhibit habitual behaviors. Any break from that normal pattern is something that a handler has to investigate. Ironically, that kind of surveillance is something that is also essential in warfare. Soldiers are trained and develop habits, and habits are something that they are trained to look for in observing the enemy in their environment. That constant examination of what is usual, regular, and what breaks from that normalized pattern is one of the fundamental elements of modern warfare as it has been practiced in recent years in fighting insurgencies in both urban and nonurban environments.

In man's earliest battles deception played a relatively minor role in warfare. Columns of soldiers marched against one another, weapons drawn. Of course, even in antiquity, some didn't fight "fair." The use of the legendary wooden horse of Troy is the most obvious example, but there are others. As several handlers have pointed out, one of the things that they found intriguing about the SEAL Teams was how much a part deception and the cover-of-darkness element appealed to them or was suited to their personalities. The SEALs and other members of the Special Operations Forces community are at the tip of the spear in developing and utilizing these kinds of tactics. All branches of the military and nearly every unit within them rely to a certain extent on deception.

From the use of camouflage uniforms to ships and planes being painted to either blend in to their surroundings or "dazzle camouflage" (complex patterns of geometric shapes in contrasting colors, interrupting and intersecting each other to make it difficult for an enemy to estimate the size, speed, and direction of a moving object) to entire units whose sole purpose is to deceive the enemy to propaganda campaigns— these are part and parcel of what soldiers must deal with. In fact, in World War II, the army took advantage of the talents of some of its inductees—actors, painters (Ellsworth Kelly among them), designers (Bill Blass), and others with nontraditional military skills—and placed them together in a platoon called the Twenty-third Headquarters Special Troops that operated out of Fort Drum, New York. In his book *Secret Soldiers,* Philip Gerard tells the story of this unique assembly of men and tactics, detailing the use of inflatable tanks and artillery weapons to dupe the enemy into believing that, based on aerial reconnaissance photos, our troops were one place when they were actually in another. They even had actors impersonating officers to deceive civilian informers and spies about the whereabouts of key figures. The Twenty-third Special Troops utilized their skills in a way that I see as similar to the way we use the dogs that I've trained and that the SEALs deployed.

These dogs have nontraditional military skills: their sense of smell isn't something every soldier needs to have refined to a great degree. Dogs are also incredibly stealthy: combine the relative quiet of their footfalls with their incredible speed, and you have a "soldier" that can sneak up on and subdue an enemy in ways that a human just plain can't. Given the nature of warfare today, which is frequently conducted in modern urban environments or in other places with natural hiding places or places that appear "ordinary," and the dog is an ideal weapon.

Put simply, dogs working to detect or apprehend aren't easy to fool. Their incredibly sensitive noses and ears, in particular, make them ideally suited for the environments I experienced in Iraq and that other SEAL Team members have dealt with in Afghanistan. The term "clearing operation" has become so associated with these two theaters of operation that it's easy to assume that we all know what's meant by that. Much has been written about the effects that modern insurgency tactics have had on soldiers. Similar to what I discussed regarding Vietnam, when you fight in an environment in which the enemy so often is indistinguishable in appearance from noncombatants, or when the locale in which the battles are being conducted offer so many options for the insurgents to blend in or to hide, our fighting men have to be on high alert all the time. Most experts agree that this has contributed to the high rate of post-traumatic stress disorder among the troops who've conducted operations in Afghanistan and Iraq.

What's important to understand about dogs is that they've given us an advantage in the deceptive-tactics battle. While insurgents, members of the Taliban and Al-Qaeda, and other jihadists have made attempts to disguise explosive odors, for instance, the dog's ability to "focus" on a particular component of a mixed odor and identify it despite the presence of other odors and the minute concentration of the target odor makes them virtually impossible to deceive.

One element of explosive detection that Dave found particularly interesting and that ultimately provided very useful intelligence was Samson's and other dogs' ability to detect what wasn't there. During his multiple operations, Samson hit on explosive odors in places where there were no explosives to be found. That may sound like a failure, but it wasn't. Invariably, when interpreters questioned cooperating Afghani civilians, they were told that a site at which Samson had discovered an explosive odor, the Taliban had just moved either bomb-making materials or the IEDs themselves from that location. They had since been moved, but Samson was right. He'd detected residue and remnant odors, and by our team's being able to note these locations, and others, they were able to plot the Taliban's movements and detect patterns and variances from those patterns. All of that is very useful intelligence in combating what was a real scourge of a deceptive maneuvers in both Iraq and Afghanistan—the use of IEDs.

As I mentioned above, the term "clearing" is one that most of us understand, but in real-world applications in the military, a clearing operation can be anything from moving downed trees from a road to going from house to house or room to room to find bad guys, with a number of stops in between. We've all seen images from World War II of men walking in front of armored vehicles and troop carriers with a device that looks like a Frisbee attached to a curved handle. Land mines have been used in many different wars, but the insidious nature of IEDs seemed to be at its peak (or at its nadir, from the perspective of those against whom the devices were used) when employed by the insurgents in Iraq and by the Taliban and other terrorist enemies in Afghanistan.

According to report released by the Center for Strategic and International Studies:

A total of 224 U.S. soldiers in Iraq were wounded by IEDs in 2010 through October 1st, or about 25 per month, with a peak in February. This compares to 305 in the same period in 2009, or about 34 injuries caused by IEDs per month. These numbers demonstrate a dramatic drop in IED injuries from previous years. Between 2004 and 2008, the average number of U.S. soldiers wounded by IEDs was roughly 336 a month.[3]

Obviously, there are a number of factors that contributed to the dramatic decline in the number of casualties related to IEDs, including relative troop concentrations, improvements in armor plating of vehicles, and a concerted effort to detect these explosives. How much canine detection contributed to this is not something that has been quantified, and given the somewhat scattered nature of the use of dogs by the military, that is likely not something that will ever be noted exactly.

All we have to go on, then, is the anecdotal evidence. Ask

any fighting man who worked with a canine team how important explosive detection was to his life either being saved or not terribly altered by an IED, and he'll tell you that contribution was huge. In human terms, if not in numerical terms, dogs like Samson were invaluable.

Dave told me one story of how Samson contributed to this reduction in casualties. While still serving with the same team whose one SEAL's gear had been piss-baptized by Samson, Dave and the others were billeted within the city limits of Kandahar. By this point, after Dave's introductory statements and introductions, the members of the platoon understood what Dave's and Samson's roles were. They also knew that, as Dave put it, "This dog was like my kid. I wasn't going to needlessly put him in harms way and get him blown up. I had made sure the guys understood the limits of what we could and could not do."

This was Dave and Samson's second deployment, and Samson had clearly learned some things their first time in country. The high operational tempo during their first deployment had been tough on them both; nightly missions for weeks on end had strained them both. Toward the end of their six-month deployment, Dave had noticed that Samson wasn't eating with his usual gusto and had some digestive issues. But Samson had come back and rehabilitated nicely, and to that point Dave was satisfied that Samson was at the top of his game both physically and mentally. He was still observing Samson intently and was glad that even though they were in a particularly hot zone in terms of engagements with the enemy, Samson seemed little worse for wear halfway through the duration of their assignment.

Operationally, the weather played a significant part in Dave's concern about Samson's well-being and his performance capability. In June and July, Kandahar averages slightly more that 350 sun hours, less than 5 mm of rain, and a daily high temperature of 39 degrees Celsius (102.2 Fahrenheit). Nighttime lows average 19 degrees Celsius, or 66 degrees Fahrenheit. Those nighttime cool temperatures plus the cover of darkness make late-night operations in some ways ideal and in others anything but. The operational tempo can be dictated by the frequency of the missions but also by the irregular nature of them; anyone who works a schedule that is a mix of daytime hours and nighttime hours can attest to the toll that takes.

In addition to those stresses and tasks—in this case, clearing a heavily traveled road to the northwest of Kandahar, a key supply line of troops, materiel, and civilian conduct of business—the members of this team were also working as trainers of Host Nation Security Forces. One of the other major elements of the U.S. efforts to combat the insurgency in those two countries in particular was the obvious need to train members of the host nation and to bring them to a higher standard of professionalism and performance. This one aspect of nation building was not something that the SEALs and most other fighting men had been initially trained to do. Whether this was something they signed up to do, were eager to do, or barely tolerated isn't the subject of this book, though the author has his own opinions. That additional role was, however, a reality for many troops.

Dave related that all of these factors were a part of the mission he undertook with Samson in doing explosive-detection work that very hot and very bright July of 2010. Mother Nature has also mastered camouflage. The bright sun of a high desert environment and the relative lack of contrasting colors between the terrain and the buildings is a combination of dazzle and blend. Again, it is one thing to train in environments like this day after day, when blistered lips and sweat-stung eyes become a nonfactor. But layer on the length of the deployment, the seriousness of the work, the irregularity of the sleep cycle, the added responsibility of working alongside soldiers whose language you don't speak and whose experience is negligible in comparison to your own, and the stress level is as high as the mercury in a thermometer.

Dave recalls the ride out from Kandahar: "We all piled into the back of a Toyota Hilux pickup—a vehicle you see just about everywhere over there. Samson was in good spirits. We set out just as the sun was coming up, so it was still comfortable. As hard as it is to think of a place like that being beautiful—it's so dry and the scrub brush and desert are so brown and tan—but at that hour, the early morning sunlight softened everything. We passed a few small villages, just a few low-slung houses. I guess that after morning prayers, the men came out and started to work the fields.

"Like any dog, Samson liked driving along, scenting the air. He was always comfortable in vehicles, and this ride was no exception. He was cool with being with me and the other team members, and he showed no sign that the host-nation dudes were any different to him. It was hard to tell how they felt about Samson. They mostly just ignored him."

Even Muslims in America are uncertain about what exactly the teaching of the prophet has to say about the owner-ship and attitude toward dogs. A quick look on the Internet will provide you with the broad spectrum of half-truths, myths, distortions, and some citations and interpretations from the Koran about dogs. These range from some believing that their faith forbids the ownership of dogs, that dogs should be killed, that they are unclean beasts whose saliva should be avoided and if it should come in contact with your "vessels" (dishes), they should be washed seven times before you use them, and a whole lot more. The situation is a complicated one, but according to what some Muslim scholars say, maybe their prophet was more realistic about canines than we might believe. They state that Allah was fine with people having working dogs: "Whoever keeps a dog that is not a dog for hunting, herding livestock, or farming, two *qiraats* will be deducted from his reward each day." But they also say, "The angels do not enter a house in which there is a dog or an image."

Given the appearance and temperament of most of the Navy SEAL dogs, whether you're a Muslim or not, you might be a bit fearful of these K9 warriors. In Dave's case, their comfort or discomfort with being around Samson wasn't operationally pertinent to any great extent; he had a job to do, and so did his dog.

After an hour or more of driving, they stopped at a check-point to resume operations and training along the road. Dave and Samson both took a good long drink before getting started. They were to clear a stretch of road about two and a half kilometers long. When they were finished, the other members of the team were going to follow up later to do a routine patrol. Of course, nothing is ever routine; but that's what the plan called for.

Because this was to be a long patrol, thirteen kilometers, the host-nation trainees set out first, accompanied by their American supervisors.

"In introducing Samson to the other members of the team," Dave said, "I'd had to let them know what his limits were. Some of the guys were surprised that he'd 'only' be able to do a certain distance at a time. They looked at the kind of shape he was in and thought that he could go for clicks and clicks, no trouble. And in certain instances, he can. I had to explain that in training, covering that kind of distance was no problem—if he wasn't in continuous search mode. Just trotting along or even sprinting, two and a half clicks was nothing for him. I explained that when he was on detection continuously, his breathing was different. I tried to get them to imagine what it would be like for them to run while exhaling out of their noses and inhaling, just pushing that air back and forth at a rate of about one revolution per second. That's what Samson would have to do, all the time taking in the dust from these dirt roads."

Once Samson and Dave began their first portion of the detection work, Dave had another issue to deal with: "The winds were swirling and crisscrossing all over the place, so that meant we had to be quartering the wind from left to right. Samson was on leash, and we headed along the right-hand side of the road, with him doing his serpentine tracking. After all the training we'd done and all the experience he'd had in the field, I didn't have to lead Samson to the downwind side. He just knew where to go."

Two other team members were on comms, and they had air support above; in this case, an AC-130 gunship served as their eyes in the sky.

After an hour, they stopped for a break. Dave waited for Samson's respiration rate to slow. How much of his panting was due to the rising temperatures and his exertion level was something that Dave had to figure out. He didn't want to work Samson too hard and overheat him. Though the Malinois would naturally shed their undercoat in response to the heat, his thick topcoat and black head, which drew more of the sun's rays, had to make him feel a lot hotter than the humans in their gear.

Dave led Samson back to the truck. The host-nation trainees needed some more practice, so they clambered out of the vehicle and started doing their own search. After a few minutes, Dave could hear some excited talking floating on the thermal heat waves.

"They thought they'd hit on something. They started digging around a bit, but it turned out that there was nothing there. The machine must have hit on something, but it wasn't a trigger or a device."

Samson was used to relieving himself at fairly regular hours, and that also was a part of the reason for taking the break when they did. While the host-nation guys continued to explore what they thought was a hot area, Dave led Samson up ahead, fully expecting him to stop somewhere to do his business. He did, but not the kind that Dave expected.

"We were a hundred or so yards ahead of the host-nation soldiers. I saw Samson's ears go straight up. I knew he was on something, but at that point, it could have been anything he might have seen or smelled. Then his tail went high and he wagged it. That's when I thought that he was on some explosives. When he detects human odor, it's the low wag. Explosive stuff, high tail wags. That's Samson's tell. Other dogs I know, one of them tucks his tail in; another poops. They've all got their way of letting you know *I'm on something*. This time, though, it was just one quick high tail wag and he stopped. I figured it was nothing, and I turned around to go back to the truck. Samson followed for a second, but then he turned back and did it again. Then he seemed to lose it again. I was getting worried, thinking that maybe something was wrong with him. False hits weren't something that he had ever had problems with."

After another hit signal and another few signs of uncertainty, Dave knew what to do. "I know that the dogs, when on leash, sometimes don't signal as strongly and surely as they would off leash. Something about their instincts makes them better at detection on their own. So I released him. Good thing I did."

About forty yards from where Samson had first showed indications that he'd hit on an explosive odor, he sat on the spot. Dave recalled Samson, and the men proceeded to use one of the machines to verify his find. What Samson had found was the trigger switch. A few yards away was another, while the IED itself was wired and waiting on the opposite side of the road.

"That was a big find," Dave said. "The EOD detail followed up and said that it was too large to transport and destroy. After we'd finished they came back and exploded it. I can't talk about the specifics of what we found, but an IED that large would have done some major damage to us or whoever else came across and detonated it, would've taken out a Humvee for sure."

As soon as Samson had returned to his side, Dave rewarded him. "I gave him his tennis ball and played with him for a few minutes and then gave him a couple of dog treats I carry with me. Samson seemed pretty damn happy to have just those."

For a dog whose head-to-body ratio and slight build was the source of much teasing to a battle-tested detection expert, Samson's experience is in most ways typical of what SOF dogs do regularly. Dave related another part of Samson's story that makes him less typical.

"We were back on shore leave, and I had him with me. We were out and about, and this woman in front of us was pushing her kid in a stroller. We were behind them, and the kid dropped a stuffed animal. When we got up to it, I could see that it was the Sesame Street character Elmo, the red guy. Samson picked that thing up, and he did that usual dog thing of kind of strutting proudly with his *Look what I found* head-high thing going on. I hurried a bit to catch up to the woman, and she heard us coming and turned around. Her eyes got all big, and she stepped in front of her baby to protect him or her."

"We put the brakes on. The lady was looking at Samson and the toy he had in his mouth, and I could tell she was pissed. I started to apologize, but then she kind of smiled a bit. I told Samson to release, and he did immediately. The woman's smile widened. She nodded her head. After she said, 'Let him keep it. That's the least I can do. That dog's out there saving lives,' I knew she was familiar with our program, living nearby and all. It was a small thing for her to do and say, and I thanked her. Samson loved that toy. He never tore it up. I've still got it. When he comes back and I get to keep him when he retires, that toy will be right here waiting for him. I can't wait to see his reaction."

10

When Lloyd earned his trident, he fully expected that at some point, he might be involved in close-in combat, maybe in the desert, even. In 2008, he sat straddling an opponent, his hands wrapped around his neck, feeling the last bit of fight going out of him. Instead of a jihadist or a member of the Taliban, Lloyd's foe was his newly acquired SOF trainee dog, Cairo. A few moments before, Lloyd had been firing his Heckler & Koch MK 23 Mod O as part of a drill to simulate an actual firefight to accustom Cairo to the potential reality of what'd he'd face when deployed. In an instant, the leashed dog was on him, his jaws snapping, spit flying, and the sound of his fierce barking a counterpoint to the sound of the other trainee's weapons discharging.

"I didn't know what the hell was going on. I knew that Cairo was a bit gun-shy, but to have him turn on me like that was a bit of a surprise. I was out there essentially bare-assed naked without a bite suit on, and this dog was giving me his best. I had to throw a few punches at him to try to subdue him. Here I was in the desert in eastern California locked in hand-to-hand—well, hand-to-jaw—combat with this seventy-five-pound dog I'd only been working with for a few weeks. Finally I was able to wrestle him to the ground, and I had my hands around his neck. Those muscles are so well developed, it was like I had a giant anaconda in my grip. I kept choking and choking, and finally he submitted. I'd been around dogs long enough to know that I had to let up immediately. It was like he'd said uncle, was tapped out like a wrestler might be or whatever. If I kept going, his brain would switch from *Okay, you got me* mode, to *Okay, this is a life-and-death struggle, and I'm going to kick into another gear* mode. Glad it didn't come to that."

Cairo's reaction to the gunfire was extreme, and he eventually overcame his aversion, to become the first West Coast Navy SEAL canine warrior to be deployed. Lloyd and Cairo's pairing tells the story of the earliest days of the SEALs' use of canines and their training for an SOF environment. I wasn't involved in the program yet as a supplier and trainer, and those first efforts were a case of expediency over experience. By that I mean that the command decided that the other SEAL Teams should have access to a weapon that SEAL Team 6 had already been utilizing. Better funded, SEAL Team 6 was frequently on the cutting edge, and that was the case with the SOF dog teams. As a result of the essential dismantling of the patrol-dogs program following the end of the Vietnam War, we didn't have access to a ready supply of dogs

and trainers who could do the kinds of tactic-specific training that we do today. So, when the navy tried to source dogs,
they turned to the civilian community. The closest thing that
anyone had to the kind of dogs needed were trainers who
provide so-called "attack" dogs, as Lloyd puts it, who worked
for law-enforcement agencies.

This is no knock on the navy or those breeders and trainers, and they did the best with the knowledge and experience that they had at the time. This certainly wasn't a case of
the blind leading the blind. The vendors and trainers in those
first few classes of training SEALs' dogs had years of experience in training dogs for the tasks that are required of civilian
security forces. They weren't prepared to, and didn't have
what I see as the necessary tactical experience to, make these
dogs the best possible partners to help SEALs carry out a
mission-specific set of tasks. That's just how it is when you
start something new.

For Lloyd, starting something new was enormously ap-
pealing. That's one of the advantages of being there at the
beginning. There's a lot of excitement surrounding the ven-
ture. For Lloyd, that excitement centered on the possibility of
becoming operational much sooner than he otherwise might
have been. When word first came down that the SEALs were
looking for volunteers, he was eager to get started with the
program. A dog lover and not someone who adapted easily to
a desk job, Lloyd saw this as the ideal opportunity. He had
no formal experience in training dogs, but he wasn't alone in
that, and as a kind of blank slate, he was in some ways better
off than someone who came into the program with precon-
ceived ideas and habits that needed to be broken.

Lloyd soon realized one thing. He wasn't comfortable with all the training methods that were being used, but he followed the instructions he was given, trusting that what he was being told was the right thing. In order to correct the dogs, the use of a correction stick, a cross between a riding crop and a billy club, a soft leather instrument, was used frequently. This is not the preferred tool to use on a regular basis if your training centers on operant conditioning. Lloyd didn't like the idea of batting his dog Cairo's snout with it, but it seemed to be working at first. Lloyd's pretty certain now that Cairo's attack on him during the weapons-firing exercise wouldn't have happened if they'd employed other methods.

"I knew that Cairo saw me, because of how I was taught to correct him, as someone who caused him discomfort a lot of the time. Dogs are thinkers, but not on the most sophisticated level. He saw and heard me doing something he didn't like. He also saw me not so much as someone he didn't really like but someone he couldn't completely trust, and at times feared. I was the source of most of his discomfort, so when the opportunity came along, and he was really uncomfortable and wanted to make it stop, he did what his breeding and his instincts told him to do: he came after me and tried to shut me down. I don't know exactly if operant conditioning, if rewarding him more or whatever, would have helped in that situation, but I think it would have."

Ironically, after the battle that Lloyd and Cairo waged, their relationship changed significantly. Cairo was a curious mix of supreme alpha dog and calm presence. Lloyd remembers the first time they met.

"We weren't given a choice of which dog we were going to be paired off with. I was given a number and then told to go to the kennels and find the corresponding number. That was going to be my dog. I was also handed an ear-protection headphone-type device. Even with that on, the noise level in the kennel was incredible. My first response was to nearly shit my pants. What had I gotten myself into? I walked in there, and these dogs were barking, some were chewing at the mesh in their kennel, a few were spinning around. It was pandemonium. When I got to my number, there was this dog just sitting there. He was high and tight, squared away like a good sailor, sitting there with his back straight, his head high, and his ears up. That's how he carried himself later, too, especially around the other dogs. He was very dominant, and I liked that about him."

In those early days of the program, the training facilities were not a part of any base. They took place on the property of the breeder/trainer. They believed that bonding with the dogs was important, so on that first day, when the two were paired, Lloyd took Cairo back to his living quarters. Since those quarters weren't back near Lloyd's home base, that meant they were living in a hotel. The other handler trainees weren't from the area, so they bunked together at nearby hotels. The place allowed dogs, but it's unlikely they were prepared for the sight of these dogs and their handlers rolling up in their rental cars causing a ruckus.

"We were all kind of surprised that after just meeting these dogs for the first time and only going through some basic introductory information, filling out paperwork mostly, we were sent home with these dogs—these clearly aggressive high-energy dogs. We looked at each other and said, 'What are we supposed to do now?'"

The trainers had assumed that Lloyd and the other members of the SEAL canine group had prior experience in handling working dogs. They shook their heads, wondering at the oddness of it all. They were likely wondering what was going to happen next themselves.

Lloyd remembers those first few minutes in the hotel room vividly. Cairo trotted in, using that high-stepping gait that the breed is known for, and sniffed around the room, checking every corner of it. After a few minutes, he settled down, lying on the floor, watchful but quiet.

"I got off easy. That night, in the room next to mine, I could hear his dog going crazy. It sounded like he was just chewing the place to pieces. I could hear things crashing to the floor. The next morning I asked the guy what was going on, and he told me that it wasn't as bad as what one of the other guys had gone through. After tearing up that room, this handler had put his dog in the car, figuring he could do less damage there. The dog ended up tearing up a headrest, just chewed through the thing until all that was left of it was a metal frame and a pile of stuffing."

Lloyd had heard about the program from the master chief, who encouraged him to volunteer; at first he started to wonder if maybe he'd done something to piss off one of his superiors. As time went on, Lloyd came to have a great deal of respect for Cairo's independent and fierce spirit. "He was tough. He wouldn't back down. A few simple corrections with the stick often weren't enough, he was that strong willed. He knew what was right and wrong, but I think he sensed that I was new at this whole deal, and he really tested me. As a result, I think in the end he wound up teaching me much more than I taught him."

Lloyd was being a bit modest. It's clear that the two of them got over their initial rough patch and that they developed that close bond so essential to a successful pairing. Like most of the handlers, Lloyd had a successful career prior to joining the dog program. After graduating from BUD/S, his first assignment was with Seal Delivery Vehicle Team (SDVT) 1 on the West Coast. The SDVT platoons are a subset of the SEAL Teams and also fall under the aegis of the Naval Special Warfare Command. They trace their origins back to World War II, working with Italian and British combat swimmers and wet submersibles.

Naval Special Warfare began using submersibles in the 1960s. The Coastal Systems Center developed and utilized the Mark 7, a free-flooding SDV (a kind of "convertible" submarine that can be open to the water like an automobile convertible can be open to the air) a lot like those in operation today. The Mark 8 Mod 1 and the soon-to-be-accepted-for-fleet-use Advanced SEAL Delivery System (ASDS), a dry submersible, are launched from submarines especially adapted for the purpose of inserting combat swimmers primarily for reconnaissance missions.

Lloyd also did a tour on the East Coast at SEAL Team 4, doing jungle work as well as drug interdiction efforts in South America. After two other assignments and an opportunity he passed on to work with the navy's mammal program, he wound up exactly where he wanted to be with Cairo. Their first deployment was to Iraq. They spent a great deal of time in and around Lake Tharthar, a large body of water that sits in the center of an irregularly shaped rectangle demarcated by Haditha, Tikrit, Samarra, and Ramadi. Most people are more familiar with the term the "Sunni Triangle," which also covers this same region, including Baghdad and Fallujah. Also known as the Triangle of Death, the area was home to some of Saddam Hussein's strongest supporters, members of the same minority sect as the deposed dictator, and fellow members of the madman's Baath party. A number of them thrived under his regime.

This was one of the hottest zones in the war, and the intermingling of religious conservatives, various insurgent groups, Al-Qaeda members, and fierce anti-American sentiment made life more that difficult (to put it mildly) for our troops there. The efforts to clear dozen and dozens of small towns spread throughout the region—often called Little Fallujah because of the sometimes openly fierce and other times clandestine resistance to our presence there—were critical in the overall effort to curb the violence and provide support for the interim government in Iraq. With anti-American sentiment particularly high in that region, along with high population concentrations in the larger towns and cities, the operational tempo was particularly high, even though this was after the so-called surge.

Lloyd remembers it this way: "Miles of road clearance. Miles of it. Multiple IED detections. So many that they started to blur together after a while. Cairo was just working and working. After a while, I noticed that he started to show signs of anxiety whenever I wanted him to load up in a vehicle, let alone a helo."

That was a strong indication that he was getting stressed. As Lloyd put it, "He definitely loved his helo rides. A lot of the other dogs got spooked in training, but not Cairo. He'd see one sitting there, rotors going or not, and he'd take off like a shot. He always wanted to be the first one on. Or if he saw them coming in to land, he'd spin circles in excitement. I'd just let him loose once they touched ground, and he would jump in the hold and sit in your seat, happy as could be."

Lloyd and Cairo hadn't experienced any helo-related close calls or anything, so Cairo wasn't associating bad things with the machines themselves. It was a clear case of the rides, on the ground and in the air, meaning one thing—the constant stress of working. Lloyd had to break that chain of associations somehow. He knew that Cairo was fine physically, and he'd noted no decline in his capabilities detecting explosives. Cairo's mood wasn't any different, either. Nothing that Lloyd could point to precisely seemed to be the cause of Cairo's reluctance to mount up.

He suspected that it might have had something to do with the change in the nature of the operation. Those miles and miles of road clearing were accompanied by search after search through compounds, most of which were empty, but which nevertheless required careful detection work. For a short while, Cairo had made no finds.

"I wondered if maybe he was like a lot of dogs. When you throw something for them to fetch and they can't find it, they get upset. They've failed to retrieve, and that's just not their nature."

Those long few days of no hits roughly coincided with Cairo's reluctance. Regardless of the cause, the effect of that delay was potentially dangerous enough that Lloyd needed to do some in-field retraining.

Lloyd had worked with Cairo long enough that he sensed that this wasn't a case where a correction, a negative consequence, was going to achieve the desired aim—getting Cairo more comfortable with climbing into an Armored Personnel Carrier (APC), a helo, or anything else that moved. Insertions and extractions were critical times, and any delays could become big problems. Lloyd figured that he had to take a few steps back from the actual boarding routine and replace those newly exhibited negative associations with positive ones.

"Cairo was, and is, a ball dog. Like most of the dogs in the program, his prey drive was off the charts. That meant ball chasing was a huge reward for him."

Lloyd had to solve the problem by returning to a previous point in the training. He put Cairo's vest on him and let him play with the ball for a bit. Then he attached his lead. He repeated the ball-playing scenario. With every activity that led up to going operational and then actually getting into a vehicle, he let Cairo get his reward. The point was that if Cairo had those positive associations with every step up to and including getting into a vehicle, he'd get over his stalled entrances. Lloyd's retraining worked, and within a few days, Cairo was back on track.

That was a good thing, because shortly after that, their string of no-finds was about to end. Despite being near a large lake, their area of operations was typical of the Iraqi topography: a few rolling hills breaking up an endless monotony of sand. The few palm trees and scrub weren't quite needles in a haystack; they were more like bits of stem in a dry pile of pale brown rice. The low-walled buildings and flat roofs gave Lloyd the impression that they were moving through a boot print, a place where everything had somehow been squashed and compressed. The area had been hit with a severe drought, and the fields lay fallow.

"This was like being in ghost towns in an old western, except there weren't any doors slapping in the breeze with their hinges squealing. It was eerie quiet. At one point, our platoon got thin, and we were moving in ones and twos. I was with Cairo and one other team member. The wind was crossing, and the dog seemed to pick up something. He was air scenting, his nose up and just kind of trembling almost, like they do."

Lloyd saw a human figure dashing across the desolate landscape, beating feet toward a hut. The other team member raised his weapon, but Lloyd said, "I'm going to let Cairo go."

"You had to figure that anybody out here, with the rest of the place abandoned, had to be up to something. So Cairo was tearing after him, and he was running away from our position, and even with night vision on, it was kind of hard to see him. I could see the clouds of sand he was kicking up but not a whole lot else at that point. He was flooding down, and I could just make out the target going into one of the buildings, nothing more than a hut, really."

At that point, Lloyd and his teammate followed Cairo to the entrance. Because he hadn't indicated any odor but had just stood at the door with his tail fanning, not sitting down, as would be his indicator, the boys felt it was safe to approach. Using techniques they'd been taught and practiced and used hundreds of times, they entered the building following Cairo. He immediately sat down, and inside a group of a dozen or so Iraqis all sat. Seeing the soldiers enter, they immediately put their hands in the air.

"Cairo could have gone blasting in there and gone after any one of them. There were women and children, a couple of men, and that could have just been a really bad situation for us. In that area especially we were trying to win hearts and minds. The Sunni Triangle was like you've probably read about. You could just feel that vibe, that distrust and most likely hatred, being directed at us from all over. I couldn't imagine what would have happened if Cairo had done what he'd been trained to do, but he had some sense, that dog. He just sat there looking fierce as hell, and nobody moved. I could tell they were all scared. They sat there wide-eyed and looking like they were seeing the devil, but Cairo just held them there."

Lloyd and his teammate did a quick search of the room, and after a check on the Iraqis, separating them by gender in order to do so, they reunited everyone.

"Things could have gone down worse in so many ways, but with Cairo leading us in there, we knew that we didn't have to worry about our access point being rigged or even someone fleeing from that location. We took the guy we'd seen running into that building, and he was later questioned. We never found out the result of that, but we knew this: the guy was alive and could have provided valuable intel to us because of Cairo. Without the dog there, we would have likely opened fire. Who knows how many other people might have been wounded? I can't say that Cairo saved our lives in this case, but he helped save some of our credibility, and we were able to fully demonstrate our operational commitment in the area. He helped us let folks know that we weren't going to come in there and kick ass and take names later. The great thing about dogs is that they are nonlethal force. Our being able to apprehend that man who came running was important."

While on that three-day operation, Cairo demonstrated his value in another instance. Lloyd and his platoon continued searching buildings in the same area. During that stretch, Cairo went into more than fifty compounds and countless structures to search for explosives. That kind of repetition can dull your senses and your sense of potential dangers lurking. Lloyd was well aware that complacency could set in despite your best efforts to fight against it, especially under those conditions.

"If you've never cleared a building, you can't know how taxing that is mentally and to some extent physically. That was especially true on that deployment, because we'd heard reports of all kinds of insurgent activity in the area. From car bombs to snipers to IEDs to ambushes, we'd suffered some pretty heavy casualties. That weighs on your mind any time you go into some building. Having Cairo on point eased a lot of that anxiety over the unknown. He'd proved himself to the platoon while doing those road sweeps. They knew that they could trust that Cairo would either hit on the bad guys or their weapons or explosives. Going into a room wondering is not the best way to do it. Cairo minimized that worry."

During that operation, he found proof that the platoon's vigilance was well worth the energy and time they expended.

"We entered another of the small stone structures, and at first glance it looked just like the previous thirty-five of them had—a wood floor, a carpet, a few pieces of furniture, and not a whole hell of a lot more. Cairo did his thing, and he hit on odor and just sat right down in the middle of one room. We checked the table before moving it, but once it was moved to one side, and Cairo stayed right on that spot, we figured it had to be under the floor."

Once they removed some of the flooring, in the space between the floor joists, they found a cache of weapons and ammunition.

"You know, in conventional warfare, if you find a few AKs and dozens of rounds, that's probably not a big deal. But fighting the way we were, in our small teams and not knowing if any Iraqi national was an insurgent or Al-Qaeda, getting those few guns and rounds was huge. All it takes is one weapon and one round, and somebody could be killed."

Every time Cairo assisted in a successful detection, the men grew more comfortable with him. Call them small victories, but they were a morale boost and made it clear that despite the large number of searches the soldiers had to do, every single one of the victories was important. As Cairo's find total increased, so did the men's belief in him and in the operation.

"Cairo was inspirational in a lot of ways. To see how tirelessly he went after it, running and searching night after night and day after day, you felt like you had to keep up with him. SEAL Team members are a competitive bunch, and nobody wanted a dog to outdo them. Plus, just having him there, let alone making finds, gave everybody a feel good. Maybe this is a bit of an exaggeration, but for me, even if Cairo hadn't had any finds or apprehensions, he would have been a valuable asset for us. Just having him as a companion, one bit of home out there, was huge for us. And I don't mean just for me. Cairo was great with all the other team members. You're out there. You're hungry. You're tired. A dog comes up to you, and you feel better."

Lloyd and Cairo did a second rotation together, this one in Afghanistan, and the results were the same. As Lloyd said to me, "It's hard to prove a negative. By that I mean, how can you know how many lives those weapons and explosives might have taken if they'd been used? Since that didn't happen, then you'll never really know. In my mind, that doesn't matter, the exact numbers."

Lloyd and Cairo are still together, though Cairo has since retired. Lloyd has worked in training exercises with other dogs, and he has an even greater appreciation for what they're capable of.

"We had set up a two-part scenario. First an explosive find, followed by a muzzle/fighting session on the outside of the building we were using. I was in operational simulation clothes, wearing headgear, but not an outfit the dogs could bite into, that is, a bite suit. The way it was supposed to work was that after the dogs found the explosive odor, they were to come around the side of the building, and we'd have a muzzle station set up. The handler would then put the muzzle on the dog. After that, with the muzzle on, the dogs were supposed to then come fight with me. Unfortunately, there was a window open in the building, and the dog caught wind of me prior to the handler taking him outside around the back to put his muzzle on, like we had planned. Out the goddamn window he goes, and pile-drives me like a rag doll. He caught me on my bare left arm with a full-mouth bite, and I felt like my forearm was being run over by a car. He caught me right in that intersection where your forearm and your bicep meet. I could feel his teeth popping through the skin and ripping through muscle. I didn't want him to release, because that would cause more of the ripping instead of just a puncture, so with my right knee, I kind of turned him and lifted him off the ground so he wouldn't have as much leverage. He had hold of me for thirty or forty seconds until his handler came and got him off."

Lloyd's wounds healed fairly quickly, but he came in for a lot of grief from his fellow handlers. "Everybody wanted to take pictures of the wounds, so of course before I could get on to the hospital, I had to show everybody the punctures with little bits of flesh poking out. I couldn't be too pissed about what happened, and I have to say I really understood for the first time just how powerful the dogs' jaws are. With a bite suit on, you get bruises and sores, but this was at another level completely."

Now that Cairo is retired, he enjoys his time off but still needs to be worked fairly regularly. When he isn't doing some variation of his formal training, he still wants to be a working dog. "Cairo helps put the groceries away. I hand him something, and for as powerful as those jaws are, when he carries a carton of milk or whatever, he never busts though the package. I was doing some work around the house, and I had a bunch of lumber delivered, and Cairo was helping out by dragging two-by-fours from the pile to where I was working.

He wasn't about to just sit there and watch me. He also gets along well with my other two dogs, especially my little beagle. Cairo lets that little guy roll him. Cairo probably wouldn't like me telling people this, but he's got a thing for pillows: he just tears them up. He also has had this little blanket that he carries around all the time. He's had it for years now, and I guess having it makes him feel secure."

Lloyd laughs at the irony of that statement, knowing that the tables have been turned in a sense. Cairo used to help him feel secure and now one of the things he provides him—a security blanket—helps reassure the dog. "He can still tear after things, but I've never tried to see how he'd do in any drills with that blanket in his mouth."

11

Curt always loved the ocean and diving. At fifteen, he began an open-water Professional Association of Diving Instructors (PADI) program when he was staying with his father for the summer in the mountains near Santa Cruz. Scheduling conflicts prevented him from making the last open-water dive, so he didn't get certified. "I was definitely disappointed at not being able to follow through to the end, but the really funny thing is that I was a terrible swimmer. My parents had the hardest time teaching me. I got to the point where I could just get by in the pool, but there was something about being under the water."

His interest in diving started when he attended a private school. For a six-week period, as part of an enrichment program, the students were encouraged to pursue an interest. Curt chose diving. Once again, he took a certification course, but again he failed to complete it. He also didn't finish his education at that private school.

"I got kicked out. I was one of those classic 'does not apply himself' types. Looking back on it now, failing to finish those first two dive programs was typical of how I approached a lot of things. I'd start something, get all fired up about it, lose interest, and then move on to something else. But those failures were more like delays. Those interests didn't just die out completely, they'd end up in the back of my mind, and eventually I'd get around to finishing what I'd started."

Curt was one of the fortunate few whose recruiter seemed to recognize something in him. He'd never heard of the SEAL Teams, but his recruiter mentioned them to him because Curt had expressed an interest in getting certified as a diver—hoping that the third time would be the charm.

"I was so clueless about the SEALs that I asked the guy, 'Do they do any kind of diving?' He just looked at me and said, 'Yes. They do.' Then I asked him if the training for the SEALs was hard. Again I got a kind of puzzled look, and the recruiter kind of stuck to his script: 'No. Not really.' Then they showed me the video, and it looked like what the SEAL Team members were doing was a lot of fun. I think I even said those exact words to the guys in the enlistment office.

"But the good thing was, I enlisted and was a part of the Dive Farer program. I did my basic training in Florida and then on to Millington, Tennessee, for my A school. I spent a few months learning my PR (parachute rigger) requirements. I think that it had another name—Aircrew Survival Equipmentman. From A school, I went straight to BUD/S. That was an eye-opener."

Curt was a good student of human nature. "I developed a game plan right away once I realized how tough this was going to be. I saw some of these guys; they looked like chiseled Greek-god statues, and a whole bunch of the others gravitated toward them. They all projected this attitude— 'arrogance' I guess is the best word to describe it—and I just didn't want to be a part of that. I wasn't a 'Mister Popular' type guy; I wasn't a hero worshiper either. The thing is, when those studs fell by the wayside, so did their followers, eventually. They saw their leader go down, they must have thought, *If this guy I admire so much can't handle it, then how can I possibly do it?* In a way, my being a kind of loner type, even back in high school, paid off for me."

Despite Curt's early habit of not finishing what he started, he did graduate from BUD/S in class 180 in 1991. He was then assigned to SEAL Team 1. He felt he had a bit of bad timing. "There wasn't any real combat in the world at that time. I just missed the Gulf War. The last platoon heading into that theater left a month or two before I graduated. Our first workups were in Southeast Asia to do Foreign Internal Defense (FID) assignments. That was okay—doing that kind of teaching and goodwill work. At least it wasn't all the same, since we'd lead dive courses, some segment-pair operations, jumps. The best part was Cobra Gold. But I don't know anybody who graduated from BUD/S and didn't want to put all their training to use as an operator."

Each year the United States conducts multilateral training exercises in Thailand under the name Cobra Gold. The U.S. government has a strong investment in the security alliances we'd developed there as well as with Japan, the Republic of

Korea, Australia, and the Republic of the Philippines. We've been conducting these "cooperative engagements" there since 1982. Initially, the U.S. Navy and U.S. Marine Corps were involved, but the U.S. Army also participates. Similarly, these exercises were solely for the Royal Thai Navy, but the number of countries participating has expanded. As a result, for those six weeks in April and May, thousands of troops from a variety of countries train together.

Curt moved on to become a sniper and later a sniper instructor, went to language school to learn Thai, and then went on another deployment out of Guam doing more FID work. In 2000, he volunteered to become a free-fall instructor. A great need for those instructors existed, so Curt "jumped" at the chance. Once qualified as an instructor, he taught SOF and other Department of Defense (DOD) candidates the fine skills needed to use nonstandard parachute equipment. He spent the next three years in Yuma, Arizona, doing that work. Next, he rejoined SEAL Team 1 and started working up to go to Iraq. Once deployed in Iraq, he served as a member of a security detail protecting high-level Iraqi government offi- cials. It was during that time that he had his first exposure to working dogs. "Some civilian contractors had bomb-detection dogs, and they were assigned to our unit. I'd never seen a Dutch shepherd or a Malinois before, and I just thought they were the most incredible-looking dogs. My family had a Pe- kingese growing up, not what I'd call a real dog, but I wasn't that into having him around. He was fine, a good pet, but not a dog I especially bonded with or anything, so seeing these other dogs was a revelation. They did more than just bark and sit on your lap."

It would be another few years before Curt was able to fully appreciate exactly what SOF K9s were capable of. Because that need for free-fall instructors still existed, Curt returned to Yuma. Finally, in 2008, he changed assignments, working for Support Activity 1, a unit that deals with high-security-clearance intelligence. The job proved to be more administrative than Curt would have liked.

"I'm a self-diagnosed attention-deficit-disorder type, and being behind a desk and dealing with all kinds of written reports wasn't working out too well for me. Intelligence work is important, but it's definitely not that active an assignment. Definitely not a James Bond experience. In fact, I felt like the relative inactivity was draining the life out of me. The command had just acquired the multi-purpose canine unit from Naval Special Warfare Group One, and I was asked if I had any interest in going over there. Once again, this was a case of somebody being shorthanded. I thought to myself, *That program is about my speed*. I think I have the attention span equal to a dog's, so why not? I loved being outdoors, and this desk wasn't a good fit."

Curt was right; he was a better fit for the new position. As much as he makes noises about his ADD affliction, he immediately got interested in every aspect of the canine training. "The first thing I remember about Odin was that he didn't look like any German shepherd dog [GSD] I'd ever seen before. I did my research and found out that the breeding lines and what was considered proper conformation had changed since the 1950s. Odin, though, looked like a classic GSD from the 1940s and earlier. He has a really big head and large paws and a very straight back. The dogs bred from the newer lines are smaller generally—paws and head—and they also have more of a swayed back. I always think of a Pinto—the old Ford car from the 1970s—when I describe how that spine differs. It's just my opinion, but that classic look, the lines of dogs like Odin, are just much more beautiful."

Not only did Odin look a little different, but he was also in a way a black sheep among the new trainees. He had been sitting in a kennel, mostly untrained, for a year when he was paired with Curt. He was a "green dog," an inexperienced and unrefined dog that hadn't been trained in any of the dog sports and didn't have a firmly established foundation in obedience. "Odin's big problem was his refusal to give up his toy. Getting a dog to release something is pretty essential. Odin thought it was kind of a game, and he was better at it than the rest of us. When we tried to trick him into giving the ball or whatever back, he always outsmarted us. It was like he had a perimeter-limit-warning device: he'd let you in only so close before he'd dart away or just sit there turning his head away so that you couldn't get it out of his mouth. Smart dog, but that's frustrating."

Like some of the others in the program, Curt didn't like some of the methods, but he had to do what he was being trained to do. "Choking a dog off a toy isn't a good idea. It creates resentment in the dog, and distrust. After you do that a few times, every time you approach the dog, he's going to think that you want to choke him off that toy. All you're doing is reinforcing that drive to hang on to what he's got."

Curt noticed that an instructor/trainer was observing from the sidelines as they put the dogs through their routine in the basic-handler course. "Every time we used the collar on the dogs, to choke him off the bite or anything else, I'd look over and see that man shaking his head. I went over to him a few times to get his take on things. He was pretty highly regarded in Germany, and he just said that our use of compelling the dogs to do what we wanted instead of encouraging or rewarding the dogs was just making some things worse."

Curt learned more and more about operant conditioning and the importance of timing a correction or a reward as the program went along and later when his interest in dogs and training methodologies increased. "That reward has to be instantaneous. Bonding with a dog is all about the dog learning to trust you. If you get a dog to the point where he knows you have his best interests in mind, and you do that enough times in different situations, you earn some credit with that dog. It's just like with humans. You have to earn someone's trust. What we might call treating a dog with dignity and love translates in their minds to one thing—trust. Start with the small things and work your way up the scale."

Odin exhibited, from the outset, some of the "symptoms" that affected Cairo, only more openly in this case. All dogs are different, but loud noises can trigger lots of things in them. Odin was not fond of helos from the outset, but by the time he and Curt had been together in training and in deployment, he was so relaxed inside them, he'd fall asleep at his handler's feet.

In a variation on *Start with something small and work your way up,* Curt also noticed something important about detection work. "When you're a SEAL, you learn about explosives from one perspective. I'm simplifying, of course, but basically we learn how to use them. We rely on the dogs for detection, and one of the things that surprised me was that the amount of an explosive being used can sometimes confuse dogs. Their noses are so sensitive that, let's say, fifty grams of RDX or other explosive ordnance are being used in training. Well, a ton of RDX is going to smell different to a dog than that small sample. So, in training, we have to work at exposing the dogs to varying concentrations so that they won't be confused. The other thing is that RDX is the major ingredient in C-4, so if your dog can detect RDX, he is going to be able to pick up C-4, because that's essentially 94 percent RDX plus some plasticizers and fillers. What was made clear to me is that we as humans can walk into our kitchen and smell beef stew cooking. We may be able to pick up traces of the ingredients in that stew, but for a dog, that stew's odors are immediately broken down into its component parts—beef, potato, carrot, onion, and whatever else is in there. That's why those efforts to disguise drugs or explosives or whatever with masking odors don't work. If you open your dog's mouth and he's got black patches, he has a better olfactory sense than a dog with a completely pink mouth. A dog with solid black or almost solid black is even better. Odin had quite a bit of mottling with pink and black."

I do know of a specific study done at Auburn University that details the point that Curt raised, and I've definitely looked at this physical trait in the dogs I've acquired and trained and would agree 100 percent with that study. I have to make this point clear, however. Just as two people can have the same genetic propensity that might make them successful at something—say they are both seven feet tall and are agile, which would be advantageous on a basketball court—that doesn't mean they will automatically become NBA superstars or that they will even be interested in playing the game. It's those inner drives—prey drive, hunt drive, or whatever term is applied—that will assist a dog with that genetic advantage to really excel.

Curt and the other handlers became vagabonds of a type, and that appealed to him. The theory, just like with human troops, is the more you sweat in training, the less you bleed in the war. He and Odin were taken all over the country to train in different types of environments—jungle environments, desert environments, urban environments, and high-elevation environments. Frequently they went to heavily populated skiing areas and traveled up to eight, nine, or ten thousand feet of elevation with four feet of snow on the ground to do explosive-detection work under those conditions. This was necessary because humidity, barometric pressure, wind, altitude, snow cover, all of these things affect explosive odor— how it travels, how much it permeates. A dog that can find any odor you want in a regular and familiar environment is one thing, but when you take him to nine thousand feet and bury it under fifteen inches of snow, that's a completely different ball game.

Curt and Odin did all that, but even those extremes and the incredible amount of training they had to do didn't fully prepare them for the rigors of deployment to Afghanistan. Even though they weren't deployed to the mountainous regions of Zabul Province (which makes up approximately 40 percent of the land), the work was intense. Operating out of an FOB with SEAL Team 3, Curt and Odin took the usual first step—familiarizing the members of the team with Odin and his duties.

"Even though we walk point, that doesn't mean that we take on the full responsibilities of the point man. That's a prestigious job, and guys wouldn't like it if you came in there and just acted like you were taking over. I told them that my job with Odin was to make sure they didn't walk over any IEDs. They were still responsible for navigating the route and making all the decisions that goes along with that. I often looked back at that point guy and keyed off what he was indicating to me. The only time I would divert them from a route was if Odin detected something or showed early indicators that he was on explosive odor."

Just as the dog's apprehension skills are refined so that the K9s are a nonlethal force, the main job of a canine team is to save lives. Curt and the other handlers I've worked with find that responsibility completely in keeping with what they were taught as SEALs.

"From the very beginning, we have it drummed into our heads that as much as we're out there fighting a war or trying to take out bad guys, we're really looking out for one another. When you're in combat, like we were, that becomes even clearer if such a thing is possible. All the other stuff—the politics of the war and whatnot, how the host nation civilians feel about our being there—that goes away. I'm there to save my teammates' asses and my own."

Very early in the deployment, Odin did something that earned the trust of the members of SEAL Team 5. The region they were assigned to was primarily made up of agricultural fields—mostly pistachios. They were in a fairly broad and flat valley, and the region was dotted with grape arbors. "I don't know much about wine, but apparently extremes of temperatures are good for them. It was a hundred and ten to one-twenty during the day, and then at night, at that elevation, it dropped by thirty to forty and sometimes more degrees. We came on one fairly large vineyard, something I didn't expect to see in Afghanistan, and a call came over the comms that Odin and I needed to check something out. A drying hut, one of the larger structures in the area, that was maybe twenty meters high, a stone building with gaps at the top for ventilation, needed to be checked out."

The interior of the drying hut was essentially one large room with a few pieces of framing-type lumber serving as partitions. Given the building's size—it was roughly 750 square feet—Odin had a fairly significant amount of ground to cover, especially after a day in which he'd walked more than ten kilometers (six miles). (Not all of the distance covered, strictly speaking, was spent in detection work). The search came up empty. As they were exiting the building and about to rejoin the rest of the members of the team, Odin, as Curt put it, "keyed up on something, and he started pulling me. We came to a motorbike, a small single-cylinder thing that looked about the size of a moped. It was beat to hell, and the engine cases were crusted with oil and dirt, and the metal had that yellowish patina from gas leaking onto it and drying. I could only imagine what it smelled like to Odin, because the thing reeked of all those odors in my nose. But he made a strong indication on that bike and he sat on it. Not really sat *on* it, but sat *next* to it, letting me know he'd found something."

Curt saw that a small package was under the frame's top tube that supported the gas tank and the seat. He called the EOD man over, who normally walked right alongside him and the dog. "He wanded it, and then the point man came up behind us. We could all see something was there. The EOD man got the package out of there, and he discovered a dozen or so rounds of ammo. The package was wrapped up in a kind of tape, feet and feet of something like duct tape. It was all wound into this very intricate pattern, almost like it was woven. Obviously, whoever had done that didn't want to have ready access to it, but they also really didn't want anybody to know what was in there. In terms of its potential threat to our safety, that package posed minimal danger. Sure, those rounds could have been used against us, but nothing was rigged to explode."

That wasn't the important point. From a distance of more than one hundred yards, through a mixed-odor vapor of petroleum and gasoline, and shifting winds and swirling dust and packing that may or may not have been designed to contain that explosive odor, Odin had discovered it. As someone who's very experienced in working with the kinds of multipurpose dogs that the SEALs do, I wouldn't get knocked off my chair by news like that. I'd be pleased, but my more measured response would be due to the fact that I've seen and experienced much more. That's not to take away from Odin's work. This was early in the deployment and relatively early in the SEAL Teams' use of canines. Like many things in life, timing is important.

"Everybody in the SEAL Teams starts out with a level of trust in you because they know the kind of training you've done. Still, you have to earn your credibility. The other guys seemed to get just how impressive that find was. They were thinking that if he could hit on that small a quantity of explosives, then something like an IED or a larger weapons cache was going to be even easier for him."

SEAL Team 5 engaged in a number of firefights against the Taliban on that deployment and covered a large operational sector within the province. Even though the men and Odin weren't actively engaged in clearing operations the entire time they were away from the FOB, those three-to-four-hour rides on rutted tracks that wouldn't fit any of your definitions of roads all added to the fatiguing nature of the job they were doing. Like all the other handlers, Curt had to be vigilant about Odin's condition.

"You start to wonder if your dog is going to break down—not in the mental sense necessarily, but physically also. This was his first tour of duty, this was my first time with him, all of this was new, and so we became hyperaware. You have to be. I would give him rests, and I'd also make sure that he stayed hydrated at all time. On the mental side, we'd go for long periods where he wouldn't make any hits, and that's hard on him. He wants that reward; he wants to succeed. To keep his spirits up, to keep him as motivated as could be, I'd frequently 'plant' objects for him to find. That way I was keeping that reward in the front of his mind all the time."

Toward the end of a particularly exhausting operation, one that saw Odin and Curt going out daily for eight-to-twelve-hour stretches of time, Odin and Curt proved their value to the unit. Not to diminish the important work that all the SEAL Team members do, but in clearing these compounds, some of the men took up security positions. They had to remain vigilant, but they weren't on the move like Curt and Odin and the EOD man and the point man were. As the sun angled lower one evening, after a day spent in fields, searching wells, and going in and out of buildings, a call came over the radio. Another suspicious area needed to be searched, another walled compound seemingly no different from any of the other hundreds they'd gone through. Once Curt and Odin entered the compound, they realized this one was different. Along the far wall, opposite the small roofed structure where livestock was being kept, sat a group of a dozen or more Suleimankhel Pashtun civilians.

Gaunt behind their beards, their large eyes shadowed between their *kufi* caps and their concave cheeks, they sat in the dust. The stained and tattered *shalwar kameez* they wore fluttered in the breeze. Curt took note of them and then asked his teammates to clear the structure of the animals—a smelly assortment of goats and a few sheep, indifferent to the soldiers' orders to disperse and reluctant to approach Odin, whose agitation and desire were evident in his barking and straining at his leash. Curt led Odin to a relatively safe distance, still within the walls, and waited.

"Even though the animals were finally led out, their stench was still there. The sound of the buzzing flies was nearly loud enough to make our conversation difficult. Odin searched and made a solid find—blasting caps and a large quantity of other IED-making materials. The EOD guy took them all out of there; it took a few trips, while Odin and I stood by. At that point, it would have been easy to just be a spectator. Odin had done his job. I'd played tug with him to reward him, and a couple of other guys came by to pet him and things. I figured, though, that if there was that much explosive shit there, then maybe there were other things around. I led Odin on a search around the perimeter. About a minute into that search, Odin got a whiff of something, and he started tugging me, and he was going straight toward those seated detainees. I was thinking maybe he was interested in them. But he stopped just short of them. In front of where the prisoners were was a sea buckthorn bush. Those are nasty sons of bitches with, as the name says, sharp, sharp thorns and plenty of them. Odin indicated on that and sat down looking at the shrub."

Curt got the attention of the EOD guy. He'd first cautiously looked at the bush for himself, but its heavy concentration of leaves and thorns made it nearly impenetrable. Curt noted that the Afghanis who were being held started to get restless. As Curt put it, "They started to look like somebody had put a turd in their punch bowl."

Eventually, they found two fully loaded AK-47s right under the bush, just outside of the arm's reach of the suspected Taliban members. All they had to do was time their quick scramble, and the operation could have turned into a very, very bad incident. It was obvious that the guns had been placed there as part of some larger plan. How much Odin's presence and the Afghanis' reluctance to mess with him played in how that threat was neutralized isn't clear. What is obvious was that Odin's ability to detect those weapons overcame the enemy's intentions.

"That was my proudest moment working with Odin. In my mind, he saved a lot of our lives that day."

When the operation was concluded and they returned to the FOB, Curt did what he usually did. He went to the chow hall—little more than a small room with a few tables—and had Odin lie down along a far wall. "Odin is like most dogs. He loves to eat, but I was also careful to keep his weight down. He got his meals and a few treats. The one thing I was insistent on with the guys was that they not give him any shitty junk food to eat. At the FOB we had a 'theater,' another small room with a TV, where we could watch movies. There were some chairs and a couch, and Odin always hung out with us in there. I never had to muzzle him, because he was so friendly. After that great find, I knew I had to be even more vigilant to make sure the guys didn't get lax and give him anything that would be bad for him in the long run. They were that grateful for what he'd done, but still . . ."

Curt rewarded Odin as he always did after a meal, and Odin stayed at his "post." He brought him a couple of bites of meat, in this case chicken. Later that night Odin did his usual thing. While the movie was on, he climbed onto the couch with a couple of the team members to get as comfortable as possible. He slept for a bit, woke up, walked around the room looking for attention—not that he needed to ask for it.

"If it weren't for the fact that we were in FOB in Afghanistan, you could almost imagine yourself back at home in a rec room or basement or whatever, hanging out with your buddies watching a movie. Your dog would be doing his best to mooch a treat, but he'd settled for a few ear and belly scratches. He'd get blamed for a few odors that were worse than those in that livestock pen, but that was just boys being boys."

Curt's efforts to keep Odin as socialized as possible paid off in a few ways. He began those efforts early in training, and when Odin and Curt were first deployed, Odin couldn't fly in the cargo hold of a commercial flight taking them overseas. Odin got to fly coach, and he sat at Curt's feet the whole time, very content. This was a new experience for him, and when he was calm Curt rewarded him. A few passengers came up to greet the dog, and Curt let them. Another time, Curt and Odin had been redeployed to another FOB. This one was larger and had an army exchange store. Curt brought Odin in, and before he could stop the woman behind the counter, she stepped around it and gave Odin a big hug and complimented him on his looks.

"I told her she was very lucky that Odin was such a sweetheart, because a lot of these MWDs aren't so nice. She could have gotten seriously hurt. He didn't know her, and that's usually not a good way to introduce yourself to any dog. I told her that next time she saw a dog she should ask first."

Odin was only deployed that one time. A change in trainers and protocols meant that in the eyes of those newly in charge, he wasn't as well suited for the tasks as they would like. Curt would have loved to have kept Odin as a pet, but the navy donated him to the San Diego County sheriff's office, where he is still at work. "It would be easy to be bitter or selfish. I still miss Odin, but knowing that he's still working, doing what he was bred to do and wants to do, I had to put his needs ahead of mine."

That statement exemplifies anyone who does service for

their country. The pride in Curt's voice is obvious when he tells me one final story about Odin. "In one of his first patrols, he was with the sheriff on a call. A perpetrator was holed up in an attic. From what I was told, he was a big guy, a former college football player or something. They sent Odin in there and he apprehended the guy. Odin got his bite, something all these dogs just love, and it was good to know that because of him, some officer didn't have to go crawling into what could potentially be a very dangerous situation."

Curt is on the verge of retirement. He plans to work as a civilian in dog training. "One of the things I really like about dogs is that they're honest. They don't ever try to deceive you, really. I laugh about this now, and I'm really very grateful those recruiters told me that I would have an easy time making the SEAL Teams. One of the guys out of that office somehow remembered my name and tracked me down a while ago. He told me that of all the guys he showed that video to, of all the guys that he signed up, I was the only one to actually get through BUD/S. Imagine that. I always finish what I start, eventually. It would be nice to finish up with Odin, but he's still got plenty of work left to do. I don't want him to have an ADD thing going on like I did."

In my mind, if that's what ADD does to you, then we'd be a lot better off if more of us had Curt's version of it.

Fallujah. Ask anyone who has been downrange and gotten near that city in Al Anbar Province and they'll probably use a lot of other words that start with F in telling you about it. From the brutal killing and mutilation of four Blackwater contractors in March of 2004, to Operation Vigilant Resolve in April of 2004, to Operation Phantom Fury/Operation AL FAJR in November of 2004, and beyond, the combat operations in and around this population center, known as the City of Mosques, came to symbolize some of the frustrations of engaging in this kind of counterinsurgency. The bloodiest battle of the Iraq War, Operation Fury/Operation AL FAJR was also the first one fought primarily against insurgents and not against Iraqi troops loyal to their deposed leader.

In many ways, "insurgency" and "IED" have become synonymous with one another. Outmanned, outsupplied, and outgutted, the insurgents relied on these inexpensive but very deadly explosives to inflict both physical and mental damage on Coalition Forces. A report produced by the Center for Strategic and International Studies demonstrates how the use and detection of IEDs in Iraq evolved. In the early months of the conflict, from June of 2003 to October of 2003, there were a total of 719 IED incidents reported. Thirty-seven members of the Coalition Forces (not counting pro-Coalition/ Iraqi Security Forces) were killed in action, and another 670 were wounded in action during that four-month period. According to the CSIS data, only two IEDs were found and cleared in that same period. In November of 2003 alone, 503 incidents were reported with 259 IEDs being found and cleared. We were learning, but unfortunately so was the enemy. By October of 2005, the number of IED-related KIAs rose to 52 that month, with another 405 Wounded in Action (WIA) as a result of the 1,683 incidents reported.

Throughout the period of November of 2005 to March of 2008, the number of IED incidents rose to a high of 2,612 in February of 2007 and gradually fell after that, declining to 1,175 incidents in March of 2008. A similar trend in the number of found and cleared exists in that period, with the success rate early in that time frame hovering around the 50 percent mark and increasing to a high of 69 percent by January of 2008. As I stated earlier, there are a lot of factors to consider in this increase in efficiency in finding and clearing IEDs, but I'm convinced that the use of canines contributed to this positive trend, as did our vigilance in focusing on turning the tide against our enemy's insidious tactic.

For that roughly eight-year period, 2,182 Coalition Forces

were killed in action and 18,347 wounded in action, for a total of 20,547 Coalition casualties due to IEDs. To put this in better perspective, those 2,182 deaths as a result of IEDs represent 60 percent of the total Coalition Forces listed as KIAs.[1]

I realize that numbers can start to blur in our minds and that it's sometimes easy to forget that each of those numbers represents a human life lost or damaged in some way. For those lives lost, the pain and suffering have ended. One of the legacies of Operation Iraqi Freedom and the enemies' use of IEDs against us is the number and types of wounds those explosives caused. Probably the most visible representation of the effects of those devices are the number of amputees who lost a limb or limbs as a result of their encounter with an IED. According to the September 28, 2010, report "U.S. Military Casualty Statistics: Operation New Dawn, Operation Iraqi Freedom, and Operation Enduring Freedom" issued by the Congressional Research Service, 1,621 service personnel underwent amputation due to injuries sustained in Iraq and Afghanistan.[2] As has been widely reported, the battle against terrorists and insurgents and their use of IEDs has resulted in a number of specific kinds of injuries. Lower-leg and traumatic-brain injuries are among the most frequently cited as being a part of this type of warfare.

The Center for Disease Control produced a bulletin for physicians, *Explosions and Blast Injuries: A Primer for Clinicians,* which outlines many of the main points to be made about explosive detonations. As a SEAL Team member, I was brought up to speed on much of the information included in this report, only from a different perspective: how to use those devices. The CDC operates from the other end of the spectrum: how to recognize and treat injuries those blasts/ explosives produce.

Essentially blasts/explosives can be broken down into two main categories: high-order explosives (HE) and low-order explosives (LE). An HE is markedly different from an LE in one regard—HEs produce what's called supersonic overpressurization shock wave. TNT, C-4, Semtex, dynamite, and nitroglycerin are all examples of HEs that produce that kind of powerful shock wave. An LE does not produce an overpressurization shock wave; it is a subsonic explosion. Terrorists use whatever they get their hands on to manufacture both types. What makes an IED an IED isn't necessarily a matter of whether it's an HE or an LE, but the fact that these devices are generally made in small quantities (compared to how many the military would manufacture). IEDs are composed of materials being used for something other than their intended purpose. Manufactured explosive devices, those produced by or for the military, are HE-based.

Depending upon the type of explosives being used, your distance from the blast's center, and the environment you are in, the effects of the explosion on your body will vary. The CDC breaks down these effects into four quadrants. The first, or primary mechanism, includes injuries like "blast lung" or pulmonary barotrauma. As you can probably figure out, this injury affects the lungs but also any other part of the body that is gas-filled—the middle ear, and the gastrointestinal tract among them. When the pressure outside the body and inside the body are substantially different, which is what happens when an HE creates that overpressurization wave, damage occurs to those areas. In fact, that is the leading cause of death from HE explosions among those who survive the initial blast. The wave can also cause ear injury, perforation and hemorrhage in the bowel, and lacerations of the organs. These blast waves—and keep in mind that all that I've described above is a result of coming in contact with the wave produced by an HE explosion and not from any other physical object—can also cause concussions. When those waves are released in a confined space, like a room or a small building, they don't dissipate as quickly, and those explosions and their concussive effects, especially inside something as small as a vehicle, are particularly deadly.

Another effect of an explosion, ballistic penetrations (shrapnel, as it is commonly referred to) is the CDC's secondary mechanism. These can affect any part of the body. Because of the type of armor that our troops are geared up in, the lower limbs, hands, and other exposed areas are most vulnerable to this kind of damage. The tertiary, or third, mechanism results from the wind the blast produces, which can hurtle a body through the air, producing fractures and traumatic amputation. The last category is a kind of catchall of any other injuries, including burns, crush injuries, all the way to things like asthma, high blood pressure, and angina.

Obviously, because many of the IEDs are planted in the ground and the blast originates there and its force dissipates as it spreads, the lower extremities are most vulnerable. In a December 8, 2011 interview with Rachel Martin of National Public Radio, Lieutenant General Michael Barbero, the director of the Joint IED Defeat Organization (JIEDDO), expressed what most troops on the ground already knew. He talked about how we were essentially in a race with the enemy. As our ability to detect what started out as crude devices improved, so did the level of complexity of devices they created, in particular their ability to detonate them. The Joint IED Defeat Organization was created in 2006, and at the time of his interview, his department's budget was $2.8 billion. He went on to compare IEDs in the twenty-first century to artillery in the twentieth century, making the claim that both caused the most casualties in conflicts occurring in each time frame.

While the government has spent billions of dollars on armor plating vehicles, robotics, and surveillance equipment, Lt. Gen. Barbero pointed out that the most effective weapon against them is a vigilant soldier. Though he didn't state this, I will: evidence suggests that dogs are an even more effective tool in detecting explosives. I think the following story offers further evidence to support that point.

Having gotten some in Iraq myself, I can offer direct testimony to the power that IEDs have on the psyche of any soldier. "Inside the wire," on base, life in an active battle zone is still fraught with threats. You may be watching a movie, catching up on e-mail, or trying to enjoy a meal, but the sounds of air-raid sirens, mortar fire, and the general mayhem that surrounds wartime activity in a particularly hot zone are constant reminders that "safety" is a relative term and that its parameters are very, very fluid. Outside the wire, to borrow a phrase from another war, that sense that no place is truly safe is among "the things we carry." Every step you take, one question is on your mind: *Am I going to blow up?*

The only thing I can compare to that feeling of being on the ground hustling during those operations goes back to my childhood in Iowa. In the winter, we used to play a lot of pond hockey. Our "rinks" weren't any kind of Zamboni-ed surface. We were so eager to play that we often went out when better sense would have told us to stay home. You'd place a skate on the edges of those ponds and hear that zinging, cracking sound as the ice settled, and a spiderweb of fractures moved out from your position. Still, you took another step forward, got both skates on the surface and headed out, wondering the whole time if you were going to fall through. Obviously, the stakes were much higher in Iraq, the impending sense of doom magnified, the gut-churning disquiet more persistent. For days on end, as they turned into weeks and months, that anxiety was your constant companion. Though I never was operational with a canine team, from what I've been told by those who were, nothing can eliminate that feeling entirely, but having a dog doing detection work in advance of your steps makes it a hell of lot easier to plant your feet firmly and move forward with that question a whisper and not a shout.

So far, the stories that you've read in this book are from handlers who deployed downrange with dogs that I have trained and known for several years. Because of the timing of my departure from the SEAL Teams and the time it took to get dogs that met the SOF standards we had in mind, as well as the navy's attempts to source dogs from other canine units, it wasn't until 2007 that our first dog went into Iraq. This next incredible story is that of a dog named Poncho, which was a throwback to one of the author's favorite dogs. He had been picked up from a breeder overseas, and he was a little more than three years old when he was first brought in. Poncho was one of the more laid-back dogs, definitely not a spinner or a prodigious barker when kenneled, and that suited him to this particular operation.

Poncho and his handler, who is still on active duty, were assigned to an SOF unit operating just outside of Fallujah in early 2007. During the first three months prior to their arrival, 257 Coalition soldiers had been killed by IEDs, and another 1,485 had been wounded. Those are the highest numbers for that year, and the monthly totals of 76, 98, and 83 are the three highest KIA numbers reported in Iraq. Tensions were obviously high, the insurgents were incredibly active (in all of Iraq, the reported number of insurgent attacks rose to their highest levels), and the operational tempo was essentially nonstop. In addition to the IED factor, ambushes were prevalent, but between 62 and 64 percent of U.S. losses in that span were IED related, while enemy fire accounted for between 12 and 4 percent of the combat deaths in those three months.[3]

Simply put, Poncho and his handler entered into a shit storm of nonstop, tit-for-tat action. As a community, counter-IED operations were of primary importance. I've already cited some of the detection statistics, but that's only one prong of the attack. Apprehending or neutralizing insurgents, dismantling IED bomb-factory networks, and disrupting funding for those explosive-making operations were also part of the all-encompassing approach to stopping IEDs. Poncho and his handler, along with six other SOF unit operators, were inserted into an area to do Recon and Surveillance (R&S) of an area considered to have a high potential for IED placement.

This was not, then, in the strictest sense, the kind of clearing operation you've read about from the other handlers.

The team was made up of the officer in charge (OIC) and his communications officer, two automatic weapons operators bearing M-60 auto machine guns firing 7.62 mm rounds. For extra security and to offer long-range protection for the point man and the handler and dog, two snipers rounded out the team. Unlike the other patrol operations that I've shared with you, these guys were tasked with holing up in a location where they could observe enemy action. These kinds of monitoring operations may sound far less taxing than a sweep covering dozens of kilometers, and that's true in terms of footsteps walked, but for the dogs' inactivity—sitting still and quiet so as not to reveal their position—it is often more exhausting or difficult for them. These are high-energy dogs, and being asked to sit patiently, especially when geared up and seeing their humans similarly action-ready, is not something they are accustomed to or like. Fortunately, Poncho, being one of the more laid-back dogs, was ideally suited to this kind of operation, which generally lasted anywhere from thirty-six to forty-eight hours. For some dogs, the assault or raid—the go-in, kick-ass, take-names, come-out activity— better suits their nature. Poncho was certainly capable of that, but also of this more measured kind of activity.

The team established 360-degree-perimeter security, everyone hunkered down and basically on watch. The insurgents used two methods primarily to detonate their IEDs. And those explosives ranged from antitank rounds and 105 mm artillery shells they'd buried and would remotely detonate, to homemade explosives, or HMEs, often made from ammonium nitrate. The other type of detonator was a pressure plate, sensitive enough that a human stepping on that plate could trigger the explosion.

With the first detonation method, a lookout has to be present to see the approaching vehicles and time the detonation to maximize the damage. Generally, the insurgents hid in a high, elevated place from which they had both a good view and the best chance of escaping to a safe location.

A day into their R&S operation, the team observed a NATO vehicle patrol moving through the area. The team also saw movement just beyond a rocky outcropping that dotted what more than one solider has described as something appearing very much like the surface of the moon. Anytime a vehicle was in motion, it was vulnerable to attack. Detecting that other movement, about two hundred yards from the SOF team's position, wasn't enough to prevent the lookout from detonating the IED. After the explosion, they did see the insurgent run to a nearby moped. He hopped aboard and started to speed off.

Once he was given the *reviere* command, Poncho lit out after the insurgent, who had a several-hundred-yard head start and was also on a moving vehicle—albeit a somewhat slow one. Due to the angle and elevation that the team was at, the insurgent was immediately out of weapons range. Another complicating factor was that as fluid as rules of engagement tended to be, and as much as the team wanted to adhere to them, their 99 percent certainty that the man on the moped was the same man who detonated the IED wasn't sufficient enough to justify shooting him. Without Poncho being with them, this would have been another case of a bad guy getting away.

Poncho soon ate up the distance between his original position and the fleeing insurgent. Ignoring the moped and focusing solely on the fact that something was moving at a high rate of speed, which he had been commanded to go get, Poncho dipped down a knoll and out of sight. The team mobilized and did a hasty leapfrog patrol in pursuit of the man on the moped and the dog. They arrived at the top of the knoll just in time to see Poncho grab the insurgent by the back of the right calf, clamp on, put on his brakes, and pull the man from the moped, which cartwheeled a couple of times before coming to a stop. The team continued their pursuit while Poncho continued to hold on to and punish the screaming and dazed insurgent. The team rolled up on them and then apprehended and secured their prisoner after Poncho was released from his target to get his second reward of that day—a long tug-of-war session with Dad.

The humans' reward was that the man being held did have a trigger on him, and he was detained, questioned, and gave up some valuable intelligence. He was also out of the conflict for the duration.

Poncho's maturity and athleticism—he was indeed moving at thirty-plus miles per hour in order to catch a vehicle moving at somewhere around eighteen miles per hour—combined in this case for the best possible outcome, given that an IED was detonated. Obviously, the most desirable outcome would have been for that IED to have been detected prior to the convoy moving through the area, but with miles and miles of desolate roads and the threat of car bombs and sniper activity in the crowded urban areas, no one could be at the right place at the right time every time to prevent these incidents from happening.

At the height of Operation Iraqi Freedom, more than 163,000 troops had boots on the ground. Originally, our troop level commitment in Afghanistan was much lower until March of 2009, when it hovered around 30,000 and even at its height, in May of 2011, there were approximately 100,000 U.S. soldiers there. Though fewer soldiers were in country, as you might expect, as troop levels rose, so did the number of IED incidents reported. For example, as we committed more troops throughout the period from May 2009 to May 2010, the number of incidents in those two representative months went from 513 to 1,128 according to JIEDDO figures. August of 2009 was the worst month for casualties, with 55 killed and 333 injured by IEDs.[4]

It was during this period of heightened activity that a dog named Kwinto and his handler were downrange in Afghanistan in the Logar administrative district, between the cities of Kabul and Pul-e 'Alam. Kabul had been among the first cities in Afghanistan to be freed from the Taliban's grip in 2001. The Northern Alliance, U.S. special forces groups, and British and American air support, in a combined effort, routed them from the city. It became the capital of first the Afghan Transitional Administration and now the present government of Hamid Karzai. At the time of Kwinto and his handler's deployment, a NATO-led force was in charge of security within the city, but in the transition, the control of that function was turned over to the Afghan National Security Force (ANSF).

As the seat of the government, Kabul obviously was of

strategic importance, and though the Taliban no longer controlled the ancient city, they were actively attempting to disrupt governmental and economic activity through the use of acts of terrorism. That continues to be the case, as Kabul International Airport, the U.S. embassy, NATO headquarters, and many other sites have been targeted by suicide bombs and car bombs.

Kwinto and the team he was assigned to had an area of operation that was not densely populated and not in a mountainous region. Instead, it was a mix of scattered palm groves, agricultural fields, and small villages. The Taliban and its supporters, along with suspected members of Al-Qaeda, had reestablished themselves within various compounds. Based on recent intelligence, Kwinto's team was to conduct a nighttime assault on one such compound.

Kwinto was only three and half years old at the time of the raid. That's relatively young, but he was also a veteran of one other deployment prior to this. Whereas Poncho was ideally suited to the kind of sit-and-wait tempo of the R&S operation, Kwinto damn sure was not. A high-energy dog with an ear-piercing bark an octave or more higher than you'd expect from a dog his size—something that nearly everyone commented on, comparing him to an enormous linebacker in football with a high-pitched squeak of a voice—he had started out to be a real handful. Initially, he'd had some trouble going after his handler and our training staff, but he'd gotten over that and proved to be a very capable dog.

This was, of course, not Kwinto's first time on an operation like this. He had earned some distinction with another SEAL element on his first deployment. Under similar circumstances,

he'd lead a nighttime raid when his handler noticed him re-
sponding to human odor and released him. Kwinto proceeded to charge through an area of heavy foliage. Two
enemy soldiers, who had been secreted in a grape-field trench,
began moving toward a position where fifteen other SEAL
Team members were. They were carrying AK-47s and were
likely about to ambush the other SEALs. The handler immediately engaged the first armed enemy from a range of approximately three feet and then the second from another
ten feet. Both were killed. Throughout that engagement, the
handler was in verbal contact with both his dog and his fellow team members. After that brief engagement, they in-
vestigated more fully and saw that the two dead Taliban
members' weapons were off safety and that they were carrying communications radios. Prior to this, this SEAL element
had already apprehended more than a dozen Taliban possi-
bles as they were infiltrating the area via motorcycles. Kwinto
and that SEAL element had clearly been very busy.

After having been deployed before, Kwinto had developed
a sense of when he was going to be asked to get into the
game. Like that football player before kickoff sitting at his
locker with his leg bouncing in nervous anticipation, Kwinto
was a pacer. A "circler" might be a better way to describe his
preferred method of moving around. Five steps forward,
right-hand turn, five steps, and another right-hand turn.
Repeat as necessary. Whenever his handler brought out
Kwinto's tactical vest, that was the routine. That Kwinto did
just that in the hours before the operation began was a good
sign. As other handlers do, Kwinto's handler was on the lookout for any changes in his dog's behavior that might signal

some kind of anxiety. As it turned out, Kwinto was good to go, mentally.

Before he put the vest on Kwinto, his handler did another kind of pre-op check, as he did before and after every mission. Though in the minds of the handlers a dog is not a piece of equipment, they do pay the same kind attention to its operational functionality and maintenance of parts as they would a weapon or a vehicle.

He ran his hands along the dog's body, checking for any sign of cysts, knots, open sores, or any other kind of irregularity. He paid particular attention to Kwinto's joints, especially his elbows (where the humerus, radius, and ulna intersect) and shoulders (the joint connecting the scapula and the humerus), checking for signs of wear and tear. A dog's rear legs, especially ones as powerful as a dog like Kwinto's, put a lot of pressure on the stifle, or knee. Their quadriceps muscles are especially well developed, but unlike in humans, who have fairly well-developed calves to establish some kind of muscular balance, dogs have little muscle from the bottom of the patella to the paw. The handler also examined Kwinto's paws, making sure that he didn't have any cracked nails and that his digital, metacarpal, and carpal pads were all in good condition. The carpal pads, the ones highest up on the dog's foreleg, are especially important; they rarely make contact with the ground and don't develop the same kind of callous-type hardness, because they are mostly used when negotiating very steep slopes. Kwinto showed no signs at all of any discomfort when being palpated and otherwise manipulated.

The briefing had been precise and the objective clear, coordinates for a specific set point once they were within the

compound were laid out, as well as the route they would take
into the area of operation. All that was left to do beforehand
was to wait for night to fall. Kwinto paced briefly before settling down at his handler's feet, where he sat wide-eyed and
watching. One of the main concerns about the operation was
that the soldiers' egress into the compound required them to
cover a lot of open ground. The advantage of that was the
relative ease and speed with which they could negotiate the
three-plus kilometers they would travel on foot. The disadvantage was that there was not a great deal of concealment.
If they should encounter the enemy, they could potentially
be in a more exposed position than any of them would like.
They would have to employ a series of carefully orchestrated
movements in radio silence in order to reach their target.

During nighttime operations, dogs have an advantage
over humans, even when those humans are wearing night-
vision apparatus, as this SEAL platoon was. Because compared to humans, dogs have more rods in their eyes—the
more prevalent of the two photoreceptors in the retina that
are more sensitive but don't conduct color perception—they
see better at night. In addition, another anatomical difference,
the presence of the tapetum lucidum—a reflective surface behind the retina that redirects light back at that membrane and
acts much like film in a camera—further enhances their
nighttime vision capability. If you've ever seen your dog at
night facing a light source and seen that glow coming from
its eyes, that phenomenon is the result of the tapetum
lucidum being present.

Like all dogs, Kwinto was equally comfortable operating

at night as he was during the day. That night, his handler tactically lead the SEAL element into that large open area, using a boxing technique specific for these types of searches. When the element came to a channelized area, a sector where streams of water had been diverted, the patrol stopped and a patrol leader's order was issued directing the SEALs to their positions in the event of contact. Despite Kwinto's past tendency to vocalize quite a bit, he was over that, and with his handler out on point, the team moved forward silently and swiftly. Though there was a quarter moon, Kwinto's tawny coat was less reflective than a dog's with more black would have been.

As the patrol infiltrated farther, Kwinto frantically began to inhale and feather his tail, indicating that he was in odor. His handler stopped the patrol. All fifteen of the men ceased their forward movement. Based on Kwinto's posture and orientation, the handler determined that the hit was directly in front of them, likely in a large culvert that directed the flow of water from one channel perpendicular to another. Because this was a raid and not a clearing operation, they didn't take the time to substantiate that suspected explosive immediately. The decision was made to alter their route. No EOD personnel were there with them, and that further justified simply marking/noting that position and rerouting.

After the operation was completed, the EOD did investigate that suspected location. Kwinto was correct. A large IED, one capable of producing an explosion large enough to likely have killed or wounded all fifteen of that SEAL element, was hidden inside that culvert. If it weren't for the presence of Kwinto and his handler, the operation could have become known more widely for the significant number of casualties it incurred. As it turns out, that was just the first of Kwinto's hits that night.

The rerouting complete and the tactical infiltration to the set point done, Kwinto led the team to the compound's specified entry point. His handler released him, and Kwinto once again indicated that explosives were present in the stone wall surrounding the compound. While Kwinto returned, the element moved to a second possible entry point. Kwinto was sent forward, and for the third time in less than an hour, he detected another possible source of explosives. The operators, already hypervigilant, realized that this was a raid that wasn't going to go completely as planned. Fortunately, with each choice they made, they had Kwinto to make sure they didn't make any wrong moves. In a way, it was if they were engaged in a high-stakes chess match, and before each prospective move, a grand master was there to help them make the best choice.

The third entry point was secured, and the team moved through a compound of roughly a dozen and a half buildings. Besides the pale moon, no other light was present. Moving from building to building, room to room, slowly and deliberately, an hour and then another half an hour passed. With just three buildings remaining, one of the team members detected a faint sound coming from an adjoining room. During these sweeps, Kwinto and his handler had not been on point. A signal was passed along the line to bring Kwinto forward. Once the target area's location had been identified, Kwinto's handler knelt alongside his canine charge, unclipped his leash, and gave Kwinto his search command. As soon as

Kwinto came into that odor, he propelled himself into the room where the noise had been detected. An instant later, the sound of gunfire and a nearly inhuman screaming broke the silence.

Inside the room, behind a chest-high pile of sandbags, an excellent defensive position, a lone Taliban fighter was pinned into a corner of the room. Kwinto had the man grasped in his teeth, just below his left armpit. His arm was completely immobilized, but he managed to fire off a couple more rounds, more out of reflex than any intent. Kwinto continued to push and grab, and a few moments later, the gun clattered to the ground. The man was subdued and taken into custody.

Further investigation revealed that the first entry point where Kwinto detected odor coming into the compound was rigged with an HE explosive—in this case a pressure-switch artillery round behind a gate in that perimeter wall. Several other IEDs were found within the compound, once the EOD team came in, as well as a weapons cache and other explosive compounds. All signs pointed to this heavily armed facility being used as a bomb-making location. That it was put out of commission, and that one more prisoner was taken who might provide valuable intelligence are both best-case scenarios. Again, it is impossible to measure accurately what this operation might have prevented from happening in the future.

What's remarkably clear is that based on Kwinto's work, on four separate occasions in a short time span, he detected various explosive devices that would have with great certainty caused serious casualties to an elite team of warriors. I began this chapter with a lot of numbers; I'm glad that I don't have to add any to those already too-high totals. For the members of Poncho's and Kwinto's teams, they also couldn't add enough thanks for the role those dogs played in Operation Iraqi Freedom and Operation Enduring Freedom. In my mind, these men and these dogs are all heroes; it's just that some of them like tennis balls more than others.

— 13 —

I step outside the house and I can immediately feel it: it's like I've taken my clothes directly from the dryer and put them on. Out here where I've set up my business, the heat is like a living, breathing thing that envelops your skin like some kind of constrictor. Somebody once pointed out to me that maybe I chose this spot to set up operations because it reminded me of what it was like when I was downrange. Another suggested that maybe one of the side effects of valley fever was a desire to feel like you have a fever all the time. Could be a little of both, but who knows?

I open the door to the kennel and feel instant relief. The dogs are all up; some of them just lie there eyeing me, while others do their morning yoga and a few others sound off, though there's been no reveille. It's the usual morning routine of kennel care, and I don't mind a bit. I've got a couple of new prospects that've only been with me for a few weeks and five dogs in the middle of their training cycle. The new guys won't be going out this morning, but after they've been fed their kibble, I'll take them out of their crates and do some basic work with them.

One of them, an eighty-pound Dutch shepherd named Nero, seems to be having some adjustment issues. He's been difficult to crate up, likely because his original owner and trainer hadn't taken the time to establish positive associations with being in there. After enduring everything the dog didn't like as a punishment, a lot of the time after he'd been corrected, he may have been forced into his crate. A young guy like him, just over two years old, wants nothing more than to be out and about. I put him on a lead, show him one of the two tennis balls I've got with me, and head out onto my property. I don't do anything too vigorous with him; he needs to digest, just get used to me being with him, handling him. At various points when I let him chase after a few balls, I give him a nice cold drink, making sure to interrupt his gulping it down by taking the bowl away, putting it out of reach in the back of the dog trailer, and then returning it to him. He seems to be getting the message. All good things come from me, and there is always a constant reminder of who his friend is.

Just as I'm about done with the two green dogs, one of my best friends and an incredible trainer, Wayne, shows up. We find a bit of shade and go over the plan for the day, shoot the shit, and think of pimp slapping the meteorologist who forecast the cooling trend that was supposed to have begun two days ago. When it's time to go to work, Wayne and I head over to the kennel. While he loads up the dogs, I wander down to check in on the other two dogs, my pair of retirees. They've been fed and walked to let them do their business this morning, but when they see me coming toward them, they're both immediately at attention, eager and hopeful.

"Arko. Carlos. Mornin', fellas, but I've got nothing for you yet. Sorry."

Given the demands to provide more dogs to the U.S. government or other customers, these two will have to sit it out today. I have no nighttime exercises planned, so they'll get their time outside later on this evening. I feel a bit bad about that. They see the other dogs getting geared up, and after years of active duty, they still want to be going at it despite what they went through. I'd like to say that they are a part of some master plan that I developed as I was developing my exit strategy from the navy. I knew that I wanted to work with dogs and do the kind of training I'm doing now, but the Arko and Carlos factor is something that just kind of evolved. That's not to say that's a bad thing. In a lot of ways, the additional responsibility that I've taken on of helping SOF dogs find good home placements when they retire feels a lot less like work and more like some kind of blessing. You know, most of us who "rescue" dogs feel at first like we're doing something to give a dog a better life; in most cases, and this is certainly true in mine, it's the other way around. The dogs give us a better life.

Given all my ties in the SOF canine community, I suppose it makes sense that when one of the SOF communities had two dogs that had ended their stint serving with them, they contacted me. They told me that these were two dogs whose temperaments and characters were such that even being placed with their handlers or any other kind of more traditional "adoption" scenario wasn't exactly feasible. As you've read, quite a few of the dogs can be placed with their handlers or other families, but Arko and Carlos were not those dogs. They were also not going to be suited for placement and continued work in law enforcement or with some other agency. The one option they'd have would be to continue to live at their present location on a military base, with the other dogs that are a part of the unit they came from. Given the nature of how a team's canines work, that would mean they'd be in their familiar place, but because the priority is on operational dogs, they wouldn't get much attention, out of necessity.

That's not to say that their lives would be miserable or that they'd be neglected if they remained at their location. Quite the opposite is true. They'd receive great medical care, adequate food and attention, but they would likely be unable to get the kind of regular exercise and occasional training that they were used to. It's a testament to the regard these dogs were held in that those in charge wanted something better for them. They believed that I could provide that added bit of care for these two dogs that had both served with distinction. I had to think about it, and originally the question was whether I would personally take charge of the dogs or facilitate them being placed elsewhere with other trainers or something.

This was a head-versus-heart decision, really. I run a business that supplies dogs to people and agencies who need highly skilled canines. To take on the care of two dogs that would do nothing but be a debit on the cash-flow measurement wouldn't be the wisest thing to do from an economic standpoint. But to be honest, I didn't think about it for very long. The SOF community means so much to me, and dogs mean so much to me, that I told them that I would be honored to take Carlos and Arko. I'd also do anything I could to help with any other dogs down the line who needed placement. Even though these dogs were government property, once they were released to me, I received nothing monetary in return. I don't care about that at all, because as I said earlier, I was one of those people who was determined to give a dog the best life possible. You know the rest of that story.

Along with the dogs, I received release-of-liability papers, their medical records, and their service records. I fully understood the need for those release papers. Given the temperament of these dogs, there was the potential for them to bite me or someone else. The Department of Defense couldn't be held responsible for that. These were now my dogs and not the U.S. government's. What did surprise me was just how honorably these two dogs have served. Having learned their stories, I was proud to have them at my place.

On a raid, Carlos and his handler were the unfortunate victims of an IED that went undetected. In the middle of an intense firefight, they approached an entryway that cached a bunch of munitions. It was hastily detonated by enemy combatants, and the resulting explosion severely injured the operator/handler and the dog and leveled that entryway. The force of the blast collapsed Carlos's lungs and sinuses, threw him several feet, breaking both his back legs and his hips. His handler sustained major injuries as well. When the other members of the team rushed up to assist their fallen comrade, despite his own serious injuries, Carlos managed to crawl over to his handler and guard him. It took some time for the rest of the operators to calm Carlos down. All the dog knew was that his buddy was hurt, and he was going to do his damnedest to make sure that nobody else did any damage to him. That's the kind of courage and loyalty these dogs so frequently exhibit.

Carlos and his handler were medevaced out of that area of operation, and I'm pleased to say that they both fully recovered. Carlos healed up so well that he eventually returned to operation status and was even deployed again before being retired at age seven.

Arko also served in multiple deployments, and in one instance, again on a raid, he was injured. He was sent in to apprehend a bad guy and was shot in the chest at point-blank range. Despite being shot, he got a good bite on the man and didn't come off of it until his handler approached and gave him the command. The enemy was apprehended, and Arko was flown to an FOB, where he underwent surgery and recovered fully. He too returned to action. Like Carlos, he was retired at the age of seven, and to be honest, when I saw him when he was delivered to me, I was a little surprised that decision had been made. He'd done more than his share of work, but when he came out of that crate, he was all business.

His nostrils flaring, his scorpion tale flagging, his proud, erect gait chewing up yards at a time, he was a template for the ideal Malinois in nearly every way. Carlos was much the same, but in the time I've had him, he's slowed just a bit. It's clear that those injuries to his legs, hips, and spine make him uncomfortable when he's been lying down for a while. He's somewhat slower to get up than he used to be.

I notice those things when I release both him and Arko, but I imagine that anyone else would think they are perfectly healthy. When I approach them both, they still have that keen-eyed intelligence that I just admire so much. These dogs and their drive to work and be purposeful never goes away. They may not be protecting a fallen comrade or staying in a bite when seriously wounded, but these dogs still want to work, still want to be of service. It's because of Arko and Carlos, and the other six retirees that I've placed with others, that I created a nonprofit organization, called the Warrior Dog Foundation, to meet a need that I saw wasn't being served anyplace else.

Because these SOF dogs have such specific characteristics and training, the other MWD organizations and foundations that place those retired dogs wouldn't meet the needs of dogs like Arko and Carlos. Only someone who has the kind of experience and expertise working as a trainer of these kinds of dogs can successfully bridge the gap between their active duty and retired lives.

Every time I go out with Arko and Carlos, whether it's for a bit of ball play on my property or on a training exercise with them somewhere in the surrounding area, I'm reminded of the countless lives that these two dogs, the others whose stories I've shared, and the countless others whose heroism we don't yet know about, have saved. As much as I'm committed to providing the best for them in the years they have left, I'm also deeply hopeful that our military will learn from some of what I see as mistakes from the past. It's my hope that we never make the decision to leave behind any of our K9 warriors as we did following the Vietnam War. It's also my hope that we won't dismantle the kinds of programs that the SOF community has built. Unfortunately, we live at a time when there are so many threats to our security that multi-purpose dogs like those we've trained can serve useful functions outside the military. Maybe if we created a network of dogs as reservists, those who serve in one capacity in the civilian world but can be called up again at a moment's notice to serve in an operational environment wherever in the world they are needed, that would be one way for us to remain vigilant and prepared.

I know that if asked, Arko and Carlos would serve again to the best of their abilities. There's the old expression about it not being the size of the dog in the fight but the size of the fight in the dog that really matters. Every day for the past few years, I've seen the truth of that on display. These dogs are all heart, different in some ways from the millions of pet dogs in this country, and even more deserving of the care and attention lavished on them. Actually, as far as I'm concerned, they can't get enough respect, love, and attention. I've always admired how little dogs ask in return for all that they do for us. In that way, they are very much like the servicemen and women in all branches of our military. These dogs are not only our best friends, they embody what's best about us—the courage, loyalty, and heart of true warriors.

NOTES

CHAPTER TWO

1. American Kennel Club, AKC Meet the Breeds, "Get to Know the Belgian Malinois," www.AKC.org.

CHAPTER FIVE

1. Alabama A&M and Auburn Universities, Alabama Cooperative Extension Service, "The Dog's Sense of Smell," UNP-0066.
2. J. M. Johnston, Ph.D., "Canine Detection Capabilities: Operational Implications of Recent R & D Findings" (Institute for Biological Detection Systems, Auburn University, June 1999), p. 1.

CHAPTER SEVEN

1. VetInfo, "Canine Vision: How Your Dog Sees the World," http://www.vetinfo.com/canine-vision.html#b.
2. Nigel Allsop, *Cry Havoc: The History of War Dogs* (Sydney, Australia: New Holland Publishers, 2011), p. 19.

3. Nigel Cawthorne, *Canine Commandos* (Berkely, CA: Ulysses Press), p. 17.

4. Michael G. Lemish, *War Dogs* (Washington, D.C.: Potomac Books), p. 6.

5. Ibid.

6. Ernest Harold Baynes, "Satan, the War Dog That Saved a Town," *Junior High School Literature, Book Two*, ed. William H. Elson and Christine M. Keck (Scott, Foresman), pp. 37–39.

7. Air Force Special Operations Command, "Heritage of the Search and Rescue Professionals," www.afsoc.af.mil/library/afsocheritage /afsoccsarheritage.asp.

8. Lemish, *War Dogs*, p. 47.

9. For an interesting first-person account from a volunteer's perspective, read "The Hawai'i Nisei Story: Americans of Japanese Ancestry During WWII," University of Hawaii. http://nisei.hawaii.edu /object/io_1153256967265.html.

10. Lemish, *War Dogs*, pp. 62–63.

11. Sue Rodgers Merit, "Combat Tracker Teams: Dodging an Elusive Enemy," History.net. Originally published in *Vietnam*, October 2001.

12. Allsop, p. 80.

13. Burkhard Bilger, "Beware of the Dogs," *The New Yorker*, February 27, 2012, p. 47.

CHAPTER NINE

1. U.S. Congress, House, 111th Cong., 1st sess., House Resolution 812, October 7, 2009 (Washington, DC: U. S. Government Printing Office), http://www.gpo.gov/fdsys/pkg/BILLS-111hres812ih/html /BILLS-111hres812ih.htm.

2. Military.com, Off Duty, "America's Four-Legged Warriors," May 7, 2012, Military.com.

3. Anthony H. Cordesman, Marissa Allison, Vivek Kocharlakota, Jason Lemieux, Charles Loi, "Afghan and Iraqi Metrics and the IED Threat," Center for Strategic and International Studies, November 10, 2010.

CHAPTER TWELVE

1. Cordesman et al, Afghan and Iraqi Metrics.
2. Hannah Fischer, Congressional Research Service, "U.S. Military Casualty Statistics: Operation New Dawn, Operation Iraqi Freedom, and Operation Enduring Freedom," September 28, 2010, *www.fas.org /sgp/crs/natsec/RS22452.pdf.*
3. Brookings Institution, *Iraq Index*, "U.S. Troop Fatalities Since March 19, 2003," September 27, 2007 (Washington, DC: Brookings Institution), p. 17.
4. Center for Strategic and International Studies. IED Metrics for Afghanistan. http://csis.org/files/publication/101110_ied_metrics_afghanistan.pdf.

© Mouce Images

Mike Ritland joined the Navy in 1996 and graduated with BUD/S class 215. After years as a member of SEAL Team 3, he became a BUD/S instructor and then started his own company to train dogs for the SEAL teams. Today he continues to supply working and protection dogs to a host of clients, including the U.S. government and Department of Defense. He also started the Warrior Dog Foundation to help retired Special Operations dogs live long and happy lives after their service.

Gary Brozek has coauthored and ghostwritten nearly twenty books, four of which have become *New York Times* bestsellers. He lives with his wife and their dog, Huckleberry, in the mountains outside of Denver.

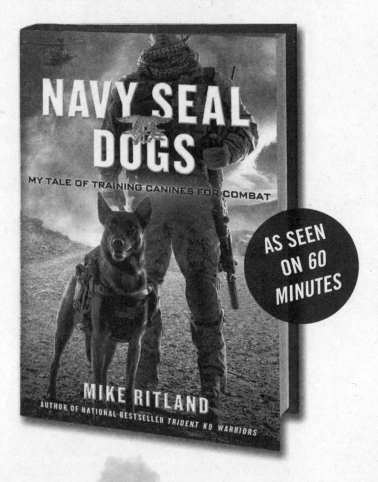